Softly Now
the Trumpet

Softly Now
the Trumpet

Francis J. Connelly

authorHOUSE®

AuthorHouse™
1663 Liberty Drive
Bloomington, IN 47403
www.authorhouse.com
Phone: 1 (800) 839-8640

Published by AuthorHouse 04/08/2015

ISBN: 978-1-5049-0570-1 (sc)
ISBN: 978-1-5049-0569-5 (e)

Library of Congress Control Number: 2015905558

Print information available on the last page.

KJV
Scripture quotations marked KJV are from the Holy Bible, King James Version (Authorized Version). First published in 1611. Quoted from the KJV Classic Reference Bible, Copyright © 1983 by The <u>Zondervan</u> Corporation.

Contents

Listen carefully. Do you hear it? Ever so low; so low you can hardly perceive the sound. But if you have ears to hear, a small smile will soon invade your frown.

As the trumpet sounds, just a little bit louder, the smile grows commensurately, and you wait with anxious joy for that day; the day when the angels of God blow a thousand trumpets announcing the second coming of our Lord and Savior, Jesus of Nazareth – The Christ.

This book is devoted to telling the story of the role played by trumpets as revealed in sacred Scripture.

And as that story unfolds, our endeavor will be to recognize and emphasize those occasions when trumpets are significantly associated with important biblical themes and truths, particularly if these themes and truths tend to lead us to a fuller understanding and appreciation of our God – Father, Son, Holy Spirit.

Softly now the trumpet, but
not beyond perception
of those
who have ears to hear.
Yes, softly now,
prelude to
a multitude of trumpets strong,
sounded by
heavenly hosts of angel's throng.
They proclaim Jesus' day,
His second coming.
They declare the arrival of
the One prophesied,
their message heard throughout creation:
"Jesus returns.
Now to Rapture His Church,
those who believe(d) in Him,
the living and the dead."
The trumpet whispers a joyous song,
Softly now, but not for long.

Chapter One

Significant trumpet associations derived from the book of Exodus

Trump-Trumpet-Trumpeters-Trumpets

Three months after escaping Egypt, Israel arrived at the wilderness called Sinai. The Lord spoke to Moses, telling him that if the people would obey His commandments and live in accordance with the covenant, "…*ye shall be a peculiar treasure unto me above all people: …". And ye shall be unto me a kingdom of priests, and a holy nation. …". –* Exodus 19: 5, 6

The people heartily agreed to do all that was required of them.

God proceeded to set in motion the steps that would effectuate Israel's special status.

Exodus 19: 9, 10, 11, 12

19: 9 - "And the Lord said unto Moses, Lo, I come unto thee in a thick cloud, that the people may hear when I speak with thee, and believe thee for ever. And Moses told the words of the people unto the Lord".

*19: 10 – "And the Lord said unto Moses, Go unto the people, and sanctify them today and tomorrow, and let them wash their clothes." ***

* - To sanctify is to make clean, to separate from sin, a fresh start, symbolically by the washing of clothes, spiritually by focusing on God.

*19: 11 – "And be ready against the third day: for the third day the Lord will come down in the sight of all the people upon mount Sinai.) ***

* - In sight, but not in clear view.

19: 12 - And thou shalt set bounds unto the people round about, saying, Take heed to yourselves, that ye go not up into the mount, or touch the border of it: whosoever toucheth the mount shall be surely put to death:"

The continuing presence of our Lord on Mount Sinai established it as a sacred place. Anyone violating the boundaries would be slain from a distance by posted sentries, and afterwards, the bodies were not to be touched.

God does not bluff. These warnings were put in place in order to control the stubborn, idol worshipping prone people of Israel. They had to understand that their God was a serious God, not to be trifled with, and not to be disobeyed. But alas, over the course of thousands of years the Jews have proven themselves to be less than ideal Covenant partners. Exodus 19: 13 is the first verse in the Bible that makes direct reference to a trumpet, or to the sound of the trumpet, - (the trump), or to those who blow the trumpets, - (trumpeters), or to their plural, - (trumpets):

Exodus 19: 13 – "There shall not a hand touch it, but he shall surely be stoned, or shot through; whether it be beast or man, it shall not live: when the trumpet soundeth long, they shall come up to the mount."

The first direct association of a trumpet in the Bible with a particular theme, truth, lesson, or commandment occurs when it is used as a signal for the people to take a certain action. In this case (Exodus 19: 13) the action is to, "come up to the mount".

For the purpose of this book, "Softly Now The Trumpet", Significant Trumpet Associations will be presented in numerical sequence in the manner indicated below for the first significant trumpet association:

(sta) 1. - The sound of the trumpet can serve as a herald of action or appearance of the Lord.

Exodus 19: 16 - "And it came to pass on the third day in the morning, that there were thunders and lightning's, and a thick cloud upon the mount, and the voice of the trumpets exceeding loud; so that all the people that was in the camp trembled."

(sta) 2. – The sound of trumpets exceedingly loud engenders fear and respect for the power of the Lord.

Exodus 19: 19 – "And when the voice of the trumpet sounded long and waxed louder and louder, Moses spake, and God answered by a voice."

(sta) 3. – The long and very loud trump of trumpets foretells, and announces the presence, and/or the spoken word of the Lord God of heaven.

Exodus 20: 18 - "And all the people saw the thunderings, and the lightnings, and the noise of the <u>trumpet,</u> and the mountain smoking: and when the people saw it, they removed and stood afar off."

While the people stayed far off, greatly cowed by the thunderings, lightnings, and the exceedingly loud noise of the trumpets, God bade Moses and Aaron to the top of Mount Sinai. Over the course of time He spoke of many things to them, information that Moses was charged by God to convey to the people.

Among those things revealed by God to Moses were His commandments prohibiting idol worship, particularly the people's practice of fashioning idols of gold and silver and of then worshiping them. Instead of idol worship of false gods, God decreed that only He should be worshiped, and the proper form of worship was to sacrifice burnt offerings of sheep and oxen on stone altars.

In addition to these strictures regarding past practices of improper worship, and the introduction of new laws and procedures, God declared His commandments governing man's attitudes, actions and relationships with his fellow man, e.g., Thou shalt not kill, steal, covet, etc.)

The importance and magnitude of the messages spoken by God to Moses, such as detailed and extensive rules and regulations governing correct conduct and behavior when dealing with a variety of types of persons, such as, servants, relatives, wives, and business people, etc., covering a myriad aggregation of situations and circumstances cannot be overstated.

By contributing to the uninterrupted privacy of God's instructions to Moses, trumpets qualify as being significantly associated with these themes, truths, lessons and commandments.

(sta) 4. – Trumpets are associated with the voice of God.

(sta) 5. – Trumpets are associated with the prohibition against idol worship.

(sta) 6. – Trumpets are associated with God's desired behavior of men and women towards other men and women.

(sta) 7. – Trumpets are associated with God's desired behavior of men and women towards God, particularly regarding obedience and worship.

And so ends Chapter One.

Chapter one yields seven significant trumpet associations:

(sta) 1. – - The sound of the trumpet can serve as a herald of an appearance or action by the Lord.

(sta) 2. – The sound of trumpets exceedingly loud engenders fear and respect for the power of the Lord.

(sta) 3. – The long and very loud trump of the trumpet foretells, and announces the presence and/or spoken word of the Lord God of heaven.

(sta) 4. – Trumpets are associated with the voice of God.

(sta) 5. – Trumpets are associated with the prohibition against idol worship.

(sta) 6. – Trumpets are associated with God's desired behavior of men and women towards other men and women.

(sta) 7. – Trumpets are associated with God's desired behavior of men and women towards God, particularly regarding obedience and worship.

Notes and Reflections

Chapter Two

Significant Trumpet Associations derived from the book of Leviticus

Leviticus 23: 23, 24, 25

23: 23 - "Speak unto the children of Israel, saying,"

23: 24 – "In the seventh month, in the first day of the month, shall ye have a sabbath, a memorial of blowing of <u>trumpets</u>, a holy convocation."

23: 25 – "Ye shall do no servile work therein: but ye shall offer an offering made by fire unto the Lord."

At God's command the first day of the seventh month of the Jewish religious calendar is designated as the first day of the Jewish civil calendar.

And this first day of the civil calendar is decreed by God to be a day of "holy convocation", a day of rest and a day wherein the blowing of trumpets is done as a memorial.

Here God establishes The Feast of Trumpets as a "holy convocation", a day of rest and a day wherein the blowing of trumpets is done as a memorial.

The Feast of Trumpets is celebrated on the first day of the seventh month (Tishri) of the Jewish Religious calendar (September/October), and is the New Year of the Jewish civil calendar. (Rosh Hashanah)

In addition to the significant associations of trumpets with the important themes indicated above, (i.e. sta. numbers 1, 2, 3, 4, 5, 6, and 7) sta. number 8, noted below, indicates God's special regard for The Feast of Trumpets:

(sta) 8. - God established the Feast of Trumpets as a special memorial feast day. But its innate importance in sacred scripture is not yet fully recognized and appreciated.

Although God did not designate a specific name for this important feast, it evolved from being referred to as "the day of the sounding of the Ram's Horn" to "The Feast of 'Trumpets."

As commanded by God, those Jews who remain non-believers in Jesus Christ are therefore still subject to the Law transmitted to them by Moses and are commanded to sound the trumpets at the designated times and places.

How fitting it is that when Jesus next returns, descending on the clouds of heaven to meet His Raptured Church, that heavenly trumpets will sound: *1 Corinthians 15:52*

"In a moment, in the twinkling of an eye, at the last trump, for the trumpet shall sound, and the dead shall be raised incorruptible, and we shall be changed."

But also, as revealed in Matthew 24: 29-31, recorded below, at the end of the Great Tribulation, God's angels will sound the trumpets. How many angels; how many trumpets, we do not know, but sacred Scripture tells us that the sound will be great:

<u>*Matthew 24: 29-31*</u>

"Immediately after the tribulation of those days shall the sun be darkened, and the moon shall not give her light, and the stars shall fall from heaven, and the powers of the heavens shall be shaken.

And then shall appear the sign of the Son of man in heaven; and then shall all the tribes of the earth mourn, and they shall see the Son of man coming in the clouds of heaven with power and great glory.

And he shall send his angels with a great sound of a trumpet, and they shall gather together his elect from the four winds, from one end of heaven to the other."

As believers in our Lord and Savior, Jesus of Nazareth we Christians are not under the Law. We are saved, not by obedience to the Mosaic Law, but rather by the grace of the Son of God, who according to the divine plan suffered, died and rose again so that we might become righteous in the eyes of our Father in heaven. To live under the Law of Moses is to deny Jesus; it is to refuse redemption, refute truth with untruth, and reject the opportunity of gaining eternal happiness, basking in the light of the New Jerusalem. *

* - <u>*Revelation 21: 10-11, 24*</u>

21: 10-11 – "And he carried me away in the spirit to a great and high mountain, and showed me that great city, the holy Jerusalem, descending out of heaven from God. Having the glory of God: and her light was like unto a stone most precious, even like a japer stone, clear as crystal"

21: 24 – "And the nations of them which are saved shall walk in the light of it; and the kings of the earth do bring their glory and honor into it."

Indeed the trumpets will rightfully trump again, not by those living under the Law, but at a time and place signaling the return of the resurrected Christ: Revelation, verses 8: 7-8, 10, 12; 9:1, 13-14; 10: 7; and 11: 15 will be discussed later in this book.

When the Son of God came to us, born of the Blessed Virgin Mary, created by the power of The Holy Spirit, He was the fulfillment of the Old Testament and the beginning of the New. He brought with him a Gospel of joy, hope and redemption available to all those that would believe in Him.

The first Adam was the first fruit arising from God's creation, the first of mankind, made in the image and likeness of God. But by the injudicious application of free will He disobeyed God, and set the human race on the road to perdition.

Jesus is the second Adam, the first fruit arising from God's plan for our salvation, a plan originating with the birth of His only Son Jesus, culminating in Jesus' death on the cross, His resurrection, and His return to the Father in heaven.

Jews observe the Feast of Trumpets, Rosh Hashanah – (Sept./Oct.): 1 as the beginning of the civil new year.

Prior to the verses documenting The Feast of Trumpets (Leviticus 23: 23-25), six earlier verses recorded God's establishment of three other feasts that are to be celebrated as days of holy convocations:

The Lord's Passover – (*Leviticus 23: 5) "In the fourteenth day of the first month at even is the Lord's Passover."*

The Feast of Unleavened Bread - *(Leviticus 23: 6) "And on the fifteenth day of the same month is the feast of unleavened bread unto the Lord: seven days ye must eat unleavened bread."*

The Feast of Harvest also called The Feast of Weeks (Pentecost), is celebrated

May/June 6, seven weeks after Passover wherein an offering of the first fruits of the harvest is required:

Leviticus 23: 9-12:

23: 9 -"And the Lord spake unto Moses, saying,"

23: 10 - Speak unto the children of Israel, and say unto them, When ye come into the land which I give unto you, and shall reap the harvest thereof, then ye shall bring a sheaf of the first fruits of your harvest unto the priest.

23: 11 - And he shall wave the sheaf before the Lord, to be accepted for you: on the morrow after the sabbath the priest shall wave it.

23: 12 - And ye shall offer that day when ye wave the sheaf a he lamb without blemish of the first for a burnt offering unto the Lord."

God completes the establishment of His feasts, to follow the Feast of Trumpets:

The Day of Atonement – *Leviticus 23: 26, 27* - *"And the Lord spake unto Moses, saying,*

Also on the tenth day of this seventh month there shall be a day of atonement: it shall be a holy convocation unto you; and ye shall afflict your souls, and offer an offering made by fire unto the Lord."

The Feast of Tabernacles also called the Feast of Booths – (Sept./Oct.): 15-21):

Leviticus 23: 33-35: -

23: 33 - "And the Lord spoke to Moses, saying,

23: 34 - "Speak unto the children of Israel, saying, The fifteenth day of this seventh month shall be the feast of tabernacle for seven days unto the Lord.

2:3 35 – "On the first day shall be a holy convocation; ye shall do no servile work therein."

The Feast of Tabernacles is the final feast of God's seven feasts of holy convocation featured in the Jewish civil calendar.

Due to its unique positioning and functions in sacred Scripture, the Feast of Trumpets rightfully deserves to be considered as the lynchpin on which God's sacred feast days of Holy convocations hinge.

Are you listening? The sound is very faint, and as yet, is only one. But it will grow in number and in volume. If you can hear it now, despite, however slight the sound, take heart. Do not think it an illusion Our Lord Jesus Christ, the begotten Son of Mary, the adopted son of Joseph; He who was born in Bethlehem and raised in Nazareth, the Nazarene, perfect man and perfect God will come again. This time He does not travel alone.

This time he arrives with fanfare, with the blare of the trumpets heard 'round the world and across His boundless universe, heard with joy within the hearts and souls of all those who stayed the course, those who loved Him beyond their love of selves.

This time He comes to take us with Him to a better place, a place where justice and peace prevail, a place without tears, a place without stress. This time our Father comes to bring us home.

Listen for the sound. It will come, softly at first, but it will come.

(sta) 9. – The Feast of Trumpets is the linchpin of God's sacred feast days, days of holy convocations, days of sacred gatherings.

<u>*Leviticus 25: 1, 2, 8, 9, 10*</u>

25: 1-2 – "And the Lord spake unto Moses in mount Sinai, saying,

Speak unto the children of Israel, and say unto them, When ye come into the land that I gave you, then shall the land keep a Sabbath unto the Lord."

25: 8-9 – "And thou shalt number seven sabbaths of years unto thee, seven times seven years; and the space of the seven sabbaths of years shall be unto thee forty and nine years.

"Then shalt thou cause the trumpet of the jubilee to sound on the tenth day of the seventh month, in the day of atonement shall ye make the trumpet sound throughout all your land."

Leviticus 25: 10 – "And ye shall hallow the fiftieth year, and proclaim liberty throughout all the land unto all the inhabitants thereof; it shall be a jubilee unto you; and ye shall return every man unto his possession, and ye shall return every man unto his family."

The sound of the trumpets would be heard throughout all the land notifying the people that God had spoken; that important events were about to take place and that these events involved every man, woman and child of Israel.

Thereby God established a yearlong feast: a jubilee year; a celebratory year of plenty, a holy year commanded by God to be free from oppression by one Israelite to another, a year wherein freedom for all is proclaimed throughout the land, a year when sowing and reaping are not required, but that man should live off the fat of the land.

The feast days and festivals celebrated by the Jews include Passover, the

Feast of Unleavened Bread, the Feast of Harvest, the Feast of Trumpets, the Day of Atonement, the Feast of Tabernacles, the Feast of Dedication, also called the Festival of Lights (Hanukkah), and the Feast of Purim, plus the seventh day Sabbath observed after six days of labor, and the Fiftieth Year Jubilee.

These feast days and festivals celebrated by the Jews are unique in the history of the world's religious observances in that they were all created by God and expressly addressed to the people of Israel.

(sta) 10. - The trumpet sound is closely associated with the Fiftieth Year Jubilee.

And so ends Chapter Two.

Chapter two yields three significant trumpet associations:

(sta) 8. - God established the Feast of Trumpets as a special memorial feast day. But its innate importance in sacred scripture is not yet fully recognized and appreciated.

(sta) 9. – The Feast of Trumpets is the linchpin of God's sacred feast days, days of holy convocations, days of sacred gatherings.

(sta) 10. - The trumpet sound is closely associated with the Fiftieth Year Jubilee.

Notes and Reflections

_____

_____

_____

_____

_____

_____

_____

_____

_____

_____

_____

_____

_____

_____

_____

_____

_____

_____

_____

_____

_____

_____

_____

_____

_____

_____

_____

_____

_____

_____

Chapter Three

Significant Trumpet Associations derived from the book of Numbers

Numbers 10: 1, 2, 3, 4, 5, 6, 7, 8, 9, 10

Numbers 10: 1 - "And the Lord spake unto Moses, saying,"

Numbers 10: 2 – "Make thee two <u>trumpets</u> of silver; of a whole piece shalt thou make them: that thou mayest use them for the calling of the assembly, and for the journeying of the camps."

Numbers 10: 3 – "And when they shall blow with them, all the assembly shall assemble themselves to thee at the door of the tabernacle of the congregation."

(sta) 11. - At God's command two special trumpets of silver were to be made for two special purposes: Calling the camp to assemble in front of the Tabernacle, and informing the camp when it was time to move.

Numbers 10: 4 – "And if they blow but with one <u>trumpet</u>, then the princes, which are heads of the thousands of Israel, shall gather themselves unto thee."

(sta) 12. - The trumpet sounding from just one of these special trumpets informed that only the camp leaders were to assemble, and it was their responsibility to pass along to their charges specific, and/or additional information.

Numbers 10: 5 – "When ye blow an alarm, then the camps that lie on the east parts shall go forward."

Numbers 10: 6 – "When ye blow an alarm the second time, then the camps that lie on the south side shall take their journey: they shall blow an alarm for their journeys."

(sta)13. - As recorded in the book of Numbers, verses 5 & 6 ^, the trumpet sound was used to signal when to march, and in what direction, but also the specific order of march.

Numbers 10: 7 – "But when the congregation is to be gathered together, ye shall blow, but ye shall not sound an alarm."

Numbers 10: 8 – "And the sons of Aaron, the priests, shall blow with the <u>trumpets</u>; and they shall be to you for an ordinance for ever throughout your generations."

(sta) 14. - In the wilderness, God established Aaron as the high priest, and in perpetuity, the sons of Aaron would be forever the source from which the priesthood is drawn, commanding and controlling Israel by the blowing of the trumpets in the manner and on the occasions commanded by God.

(sta) 15. - Throughout the generations of Israel, (those living under the Law of Moses) are as fully obligated to obey the trumpet's commands, blown by the priests of Aaron, as they are the laws of Moses given by God.

Numbers

10: 9 – "And if ye go to war in your land against the enemy that oppresseth you, then ye shall blow an alarm with the <u>trumpets</u>; and ye shall be remembered before the Lord your God, and ye shall be saved from your enemies."

(sta) 16. - When Israel goes to war in their own land against their oppressors, if the trumpets are blown by Aaron's priests, and in a manner obedient to God's specific instruction, God will look on Israel with favor and will save them.

Numbers 10: 10 – "Also in the day of your gladness, and In your solemn days, and in the beginnings of your months, ye shall blow with the <u>trumpets</u> over your burnt offerings, and over the sacrifices of your peace offering; that they may be to you for a memorial before your God: I am the Lord your God."

And so ends Chapter Three.

Chapter three yields six significant trumpet associations:

(sta) 11. - At God's command two special trumpets of silver were to be made for two special purposes: Calling the camp to assemble in front of the Tabernacle, and informing the camp when it was time to move.

(sta) 12. - The trumpet sounding from just one of these special trumpets informed that only the camp leaders were to assemble, and it was their responsibility to pass along to their charges specific, and/or additional information.

*(sta)13. - As recorded in the book of Numbers, verses 5 &
6 ^, the trumpet sound was used to signal when to march,
and in what direction, but also the specific order of march.*

*(sta) 14. - In the wilderness, God established Aaron as the high
priest, and in perpetuity, the sons of Aaron would be forever
the source from which the priesthood is drawn, commanding
and controlling Israel by the blowing of the trumpets in the
manner and on the occasions commanded by God.*

*(sta) 15. - Throughout the generations of Israel, (those living
under the Law of Moses) are as fully obligated to obey the
trumpet's commands, blown by the priests of Aaron, as they
are the laws of Moses given by God.*

*(sta) 16. - When Israel goes to war in their own land against
their oppressors, if the trumpets are blown by Aaron's priests,
and in a manner obedient to God's specific instruction, God
will look on Israel with favor and will save them.*

Notes and Reflections

_____
_____
_____
_____
_____
_____
_____
_____
_____
_____
_____
_____
_____
_____
_____
_____
_____
_____
_____
_____
_____
_____
_____
_____
_____
_____
_____
_____
_____
_____
_____
_____
_____

Chapter Four

God's Chosen People

Just a quick-look, a cursory overview of the Bible leaves little doubt that the Jews are God's chosen people,

But it takes not much more of an intensive study of the good book to conclude that throughout the ages Israel has been fickle and stubborn in their relationship with the Almighty. The Israeli's frequent return to idol worship, and the resulting concurrent rejection of Jesus are the two most serious examples of their injudicious application of the two-edged sword called free will. Time and time again, they disappointed and rejected our Creator God who chose them as His own.

On the other hand:

The above mention of the unfortunate history of the Jews brings to mind an old saying of uncertain origin: "There but for the grace of God go I." The writer of this present work, "Softly Now The Trumpet", frequently ponders the question of whether any population of the human race has demonstrated a propensity for behavior superior to that of the Jews? I think the answer is otherwise. All of us have repeatedly failed to live up to the standards desired for us by God. Also I have serious doubts that if Jesus walked the earth today that He would be welcomed with open arms by the religious elite. In fact, if Jesus walked the earth today, I don't think He would be walking very long.

Not to beat a dead horse anymore than I already have, but it is worth remembering that all of us, Jew and Gentile alike have failed our God. It is only because of the grace and glory of our Lord Jesus Christ that we who believe in Him are saved.

And God has not given up on the Jews. When Jesus comes again to judge the living and the dead, the remnant of the Jews gathered together from the four corners of the earth will finally relent; their eyes will be opened to see the light, their ears will be unstopped to hear the truth, and their hearts will be softened to acknowledge Jesus as the Christ, the One they had waited for, the Anointed One.

The following verses of Scripture and accompanying commentary – (enclosed within triple brackets: ((()))), are offered in support of the foregoing statement regarding the history of the Jews:

(((Zechariah 12: 10 – "And I will pour upon the house of David, and upon the inhabitants of Jerusalem, the spirit of grace and supplications: and they shall look upon me whom they have <u>pierced</u>, and they shall mourn for him, as one mourneth for his only son, and shall be in bitterness for him, as done is in bitterness for his first-born."

John 19: 37 – "And again another scripture saith, They shall look on Him whom they <u>pierced</u>."

Ezekiel 39: 29 – "Neither will I hide my face any more from them: for I have poured out my spirit upon the house of Israel, saith the Lord God."

<u>*Joel 2: 28-32*</u>

2: 28 – "And it shall come to pass afterward, that I will pour out my spirit upon all flesh; and your sons and your daughters shall prophesy, and your young men shall see visions:"

2: 29 – "And also upon the servants and upon the handmaids in those days will I pour out my spirit."

2: 30 – "And I will show wonders in the heavens and in the earth, blood, and fire, and pillars of smoke."

2: 31 – "The sun shall be turned into darkness, and the moon into blood, before the great and the terrible day of the Lord come.

2: 32 – "And it shall come to pass that whosoever shall call on the name of the Lord shall be delivered; for in mount Zion and in Jerusalem shall be deliverance, as the Lord hath said, and in the remnant whom the Lord shall call."

Even then, in the time of the end of this age, the spirit of the Lord will pour out upon the remnant of the Jews, and upon all those who call on the name of the Lord.

In the New Testament, Paul's letter to the Romans (Romans 11: 25-27) he speaks of God's unbreakable promise to the people of Israel:

Romans 11: 25-27

11: 25 – "For I would not brethren, that ye should be ignorant of this mystery, lest ye should be wise in your own conceits; that blindness In part is happened to Israel, until the fullness of the Gentiles be come in. And so all Israel shall be saved: as it is written, There shall come out of Zion the Deliverer, and shall turn away ungodliness from Jacob. For this is my covenant unto them, when I shall take away their sin."

Yes Israel is blind to the truth of the Messiah, Jesus of Nazareth who is ever faithful to His covenant with them. When Jesus comes again He will take away the sins of the sorrowful and repentant Jews. As a nation Israel will be saved. The remnant will repent, and will have their sins taken away. Not every Jew accepts Jesus, not every Jew is saved.

Chapter seven of "Revelation" (the final book of the New Testament and the conclusion of the holy Bible) contains the final verses presented here in support of the previous statement regarding the history of the Jews.

Verses 1 through 8 refer to the saving of the 144,000 – (the remnant of the Jews).

Revelation 7: 1, 2, 3, 4

7: 1 – "And after these things I saw four angels standing on the four corners of the earth, holding the four winds of the earth, that the wind should not blow on the earth, nor on the sea, nor on any tree."

7: 2 – "And I saw another angel ascending from the east, having the seal of the living God: and he cried with a loud voice to the four angels, to whom it was given to hurt the earth and the sea,"

7: 3 – "Saying, Hurt not the earth, neither the sea, nor the trees, till we have sealed the servants of our God in their foreheads." *

* - "Sealed" can be thought of as a physical reality such as the seal of a ring, or as a figure of speech to spiritually identify, mark or designate those chosen by God for a special purpose or honor.

7: 4 – "And I heard the number of them which were sealed: and there were sealed a hundred and forty and four thousand of all the tribes of the children of Israel."

Revelation, chapter 7, verses 5 through 8 identify the twelve tribes of Israel that are sealed, twelve thousand from each tribe: Judah, Reuben, Gad, Asher, Naphtali, Manasseh, Simeon, Levi, Issachar, Zebulun, Joseph, and Benjamin.

Verses 9 through 17 (not presented here) speak about the vast multitudes of believers including those who had gone to their rest in hope of rising again, and those who survive the Tribulation with their faith uncorrupted, their sins nullified by the redeeming flush of Jesus' shed blood.)))

And so ends Chapter Four.

Chapter four yields no significant trumpet associations.

Notes and Reflections

_____
_____
_____
_____
_____
_____
_____
_____
_____
_____
_____
_____
_____
_____
_____
_____
_____
_____
_____
_____
_____
_____
_____
_____
_____
_____
_____
_____
_____

Chapter Five

Significant trumpet associations derived from the book of Numbers

As we continue to investigate the role trumpets play in the Bible, the feeling grows that it is God's intention to instill in the Jews (and later, perhaps in all believers in Jesus Christ) a reverential respect for trumpets; not of course amounting to idol worship, but certainly worthy of profound respect for the important uses that God puts them to.

Numbers 29: 1 – "And in the seventh month, on the first day of the month, ye shall have a holy convocation; ye shall do no servile work: it is a day of blowing the <u>trumpets</u> unto you."

(sta)17. - The trumpets served the Jews as their memorial to God, a reminder to them that He is their Lord and their God.

Numbers 31: 6 – "And Moses sent them to the war, a thousand of every tribe, them and Phinehas the son of Eleazar the priest, to the war, with the holy instruments, and the <u>trumpets</u> to blow in his hand."

The feast of Trumpets was one of three festivals that occurred in the seventh month (Tishri, September/

October). It was to be a sabbath, or day of rest, when trumpets were blown to assemble the congregation (Num. 10: 10)*

It signaled the beginning of the civil new year, Rosh Hashanah. In the postexilic period, the Torah was generally read in public in an atmosphere of rejoicing and celebration. The people were reminded of God's mercies, which would sustain them through the new year if they obeyed His covenant.))

Numbers 10: 10 – "Also in your day of gladness, and in your solemn days, and in the beginnings of your months, ye shall blow with the trumpets over your burnt offerings, and over the sacrifices of your peace offerings; that they may be to you for a memorial before your God: I am the Lord your God."

In addition to serving as signals to assemble, march, commence war and celebrate sacred feast days of holy convocations, the sound of the trumpets served as clear and frequent reminders to the people of Israel that their God is the God of "I am", the God of creation, the one and only true God who must be worshiped, and that any and all other so called gods are false.

(sta) 18. – The sounds of the trumpets served the people of Israel as signals to assemble, march, commence war and celebrate sacred feast days of holy convocations.

And so ends Chapter Five.

Chapter five yields two significant trumpet associations:

(sta)17. - The trumpets served the Jews as their memorial to God, a reminder to them that He is their Lord and their God.

(sta) 18. – The sounds of the trumpets served the people of Israel as signals to assemble, march, commence war and celebrate sacred feast days of holy convocations.

Notes and Reflections

_____
_____
_____
_____
_____
_____
_____
_____
_____
_____
_____
_____
_____
_____
_____
_____
_____
_____
_____
_____
_____
_____
_____
_____
_____
_____
_____
_____

Chapter Six

Significant trumpet associations derived from the book of Joshua.

The Old Testament book of Joshua informs of various aspects of the Exodus, Israel's forty years wandering in the wilderness, the death of Moses, the crossing of the river Jordan, the battle and destruction of Jericho, the distribution of the land promised to Israel's fathers, and the death and burial of Joshua.

Joshua, Chapter 6, verses 6 through 27 tell the story of the fall of Jericho and in doing so demonstrate the important role that certain numbers play in the Bible:

The fall of Jericho

Joshua 6: 1, 2, 3, 4

6: 1 – "Now Jericho was straitly shut up because of the children of Israel: none went out, and none came in."

6: 2 – "And the Lord said unto Joshua, See, I have given into thine hand Jericho, and the king thereof, and the mighty men of valour."

6: 3 – "And ye shall compass the city, all ye men of war, and go round about the city once. Thus shalt thou do six days."

6: 4 - "And seven priests shall bear before the ark seven <u>trumpets</u> of ram's horns: and the seventh day ye shall compass the city seven times, and the priests shall blow with the <u>trumpets</u>."

(sta) 19. – The beginning of the fall of Jericho starts when Israel complies with God's puzzling command to initiate a battle campaign featuring the blare of trumpets as the chief weaponry.

The battle of Jericho was not only a physical battle for the conquest of a mighty Canaanite city; it also served as a strong spiritual affirmation of Israel's choice to worship the one true God. *

* - Throughout the ages, Israel has not always held true to that choice, but the correctness of the affirmation remains forever.

Joshua 6: 5 – "And it shall come to pass, that when they make a long blast with the ram's horn, and when ye hear the sound of the <u>trumpet</u>, all the people shall shout with a great shout; and the wall of the city shall fall down flat, and the people shall ascend up every man straight before him."

Joshua 6: 6 – "And Joshua the son of Nun called the priests, and said unto them, Take up the ark of the covenant, and let seven priests bear seven <u>trumpets</u> of ram's horns before the ark of the Lord."

Joshua 6: 7 – "And he said unto the people, Pass on, and compass the city, and let him that is armed pass on before the ark of the Lord."

(sta) 20. - In order for God's perfect plan for the taking of Jericho to succeed, the people of Israel were required to follow the plan exactly, including the blaring of the trumpets, and the great shouts of the people.

Joshua 6: 8 – "And it came to pass, when Joshua had spoken unto the people, that the seven priests bearing the seven trumpets of rams' horns passed on before the Lord, and blew with the trumpets: and the ark of the covenant of the Lord followed them."

Joshua 6: 9 – "And the armed men went before the priests that blew with the trumpets, and the rearward came after the ark, the priests going on, and blowing with the trumpets."

Joshua6: 10 – "And Joshua had commanded the people, saying, Ye shall not shout, nor make any noise with your voice, neither shall any word proceed out of your mouth, until the day I bid you to shout; then shall ye shout."

Joshua 6: 11 – "So the ark of the Lord compassed the city, going about it once: and they came into the camp, and lodged in the camp."

Joshua 6: 12 – "And Joshua rose early in the morning, and the priests took up the ark of the Lord."

Joshua 6: 13 – "And seven priests bearing seven trumpets of ram's horns before the ark of the Lord went on continually, and blew with the trumpets: and the armed men went before *them; but the rearward came after the ark of the Lord, the priests going on, and blowing with the <u>trumpets</u>.*

Joshua 6: 14 – "And the second day they compassed the city once, and returned into the camp: so they did six days."

Joshua 6: 15 – "And it came to pass on the seventh day, that they rose early about the dawning of the day, and compassed the city after the same manner seven times: only on that day they compassed the city seven times."

Joshua 6: 16 – "And it came to pass at the seventh time, when the priests blew with the <u>trumpets</u>, Joshua said unto the people, Shout; for the Lord hath given you the city."

Joshua 6: 17 – "And the city shall be accursed, even it, and all that are therein, to the Lord: only Rehab the harlot shall live, she and all that are with her in the house, because she hid the messengers that we sent."

Joshua 6: 18 – "And ye, in any wise keep yourselves from the accursed thing, lest ye make yourselves accursed, when ye take of the accursed thing and make the camp of Israel a curse, and trouble it."

Joshua 6: 19 – "But all the silver, and gold, and vessels of brass and iron, are consecrated unto the Lord: they shall come into the treasury of the Lord."

Joshua 6: 20 – "So the people shouted when the priests blew with the <u>trumpets</u>: and it came to pass, when the people heard the sound of the <u>trumpet,</u> and the people shouted with a great shout, that the wall fell down flat, so that the people *went up into the city, every man straight before him, and they took the city."*

In the case of Jericho the seventh day was the day designated by God to bear the fruit of the previous six-day campaign against Jericho. Again the blaring of the ram's-horns trumpets, coupled this time with the unified shouting of the children of Israel, caused the walls of Jericho to tumble. The perfect victory at Jericho was achieved and completeness realized due to the spiritual factor of 'God's will be done'.

*Joshua 6: 21 – "And they utterly destroyed all that was in the city, both man and women, young and old, and ox, and sheep, and ass, with the edge of the sword." ***

* - But In obedience to God's command, Joshua spared Rehab and those in her house.

Question: Without divine influence, could the trumpets sound over several days, combined with the shouts of the people have been sufficient to bring down the walls of Jericho? *

* - (sta) 21. - Combined with complete and specific obedience to God's commands, the great blare of the trumpets magnified by the deafening screams of the people brought down the walls of Jericho.

But more importantly, because it was God's will that they fall, the walls of Jericho did fall. The people and the troops, the priests and Joshua, and the trumpets served God's purpose, teaching two valuable lessons: With God all things are possible, but without God all roads lead to disaster.

(sta) 22. - Throughout the long tragic years that have passed since the walls of Jericho succumbed to the power of God's trumpets, had Israel continued in unswerving obedience to His will, its history would depict a more joyful, inspirational journey. When Jesus came to them in love and forgiveness two thousand years ago, instead of rejecting their Messiah, they would have embraced him. Instead of slapping him and spitting on him, they would have opened their hearts and minds to the Holy Spirit, and instead of arranging for his death on the cross, they would have worshiped and glorified Jesus as the rightful heir to the throne of David and the Messiah they had long waited for.

But that is not the road they traveled, those are not the decisions they made. As a result, when Jesus comes again, only a remnant of Israel will be there to finally say, "My Lord and my God."

As previously noted, Joshua, chapter 6, verses 1 through 21 tell the story of the tumbling down of the walls of Jericho and the destruction of that Canaanite fortress city.

If one reads the story of Jericho through a prism of appreciation of the reality that certain numbers are consistently and significantly associated with specific biblical themes, truths, lessons, and commandments, it becomes apparent that the number 7 played an important role in the fall of Jericho:

Seven is used to count the number of priests –(Four times)

Seven is used to count the number of trumpets – (four times)

Seven is used to indicate the number of occasions when the army of Israel encompassed Jericho - (four times)

The phrase "seventh day" is used (Two times) to indicate when an action is taking place.

In all of the instances above, while God accomplished His plan for the defeat of Jericho, the number 7 is directly linked with verses that refer to particular themes, truths, lessons, or commandments.

I think it is fair to surmise that, had Israel continued on the path of obedience to God's will after the fall of Jericho, God's desire for their salvation in this present age, (the church age, the age of second chances), would have been the reality when Jesus came, but because of her free-will worship of worldly gods, and rejection of salvation, Israel must now wait until Jesus comes again.

(sta) 23. - Although it is not stated specifically and is a conclusion arrived at by extrapolation of peripheral information, trumpets significantly emphasize that in order for Israel to survive as a nation, it must obey God.

(sta) 24. – Trumpets are a reminder that God is complete and perfect. As a collateral benefit of God's completeness and perfection, we can conclude that his plan for our salvation is also complete and perfect.

(sta) 25. – Trumpets played a significant role in the battle of Jericho, a battle of both military and spiritual importance.

And so ends Chapter Six.

Chapter Six yields 7 significant trumpet associations:

(sta) 19. – The beginning of the fall of Jericho starts when Israel complies with God's puzzling command to initiate a battle campaign featuring the blare of trumpets as the chief weaponry.

(sta) 20. - In order for God's perfect plan for the taking of Jericho to succeed, the people of Israel were required to follow the plan exactly, including the blaring of the trumpets, and the great shouts of the people.

(sta) 21. - Combined with complete and specific obedience to God's commands, the great blare of the trumpets magnified by the deafening screams of the people brought down the walls of Jericho.

But more importantly, because it was God's will that they fall, the walls of Jericho did fall. The people and the troops, the priests and Joshua, and the trumpets served God's purpose, teaching two valuable lessons: With God all things are possible, but without God all roads lead to disaster.

(sta) 22. - Throughout the long tragic years that have passed since the walls of Jericho succumbed to the power of God's trumpets, had Israel continued in unswerving obedience to His will, the history of Israel would depict a more joyful, inspirational journey. When Jesus came to them in love and forgiveness two thousand years ago, instead of rejecting their Messiah, they would have embraced him. Instead of slapping him and spitting on him, they would have opened their hearts and minds to the Holy Spirit, and instead of arranging for his death on the cross, they would have worshiped and

glorified Jesus as the rightful heir to the throne of David and the Messiah they had long waited for.

But that is not the road they traveled, those are not the decisions they made. And as a result, when Jesus comes again, only a remnant of Israel will be there to finally say, "My Lord and my God."

(sta) 23. - Although it is not stated specifically and is a conclusion arrived at by extrapolation of peripheral information, trumpets significantly emphasize that in order for Israel to survive as a nation, it must obey God.

(sta) 24. – Trumpets are a reminder that God is complete and perfect. As a collateral benefit of God's completeness and perfection, we can conclude that his plan for our salvation is also complete and perfect.

(sta) 25. – Trumpets played a significant role in the battle of Jericho, a battle of both military and spiritual importance.

Notes and Reflections

Chapter Seven

Significant trumpet associations derived from the book of Judges.

The next group of verses relates the story of Israel's victory over Eglon the king of the Moabites. This victory serves as a prime example of the frequent intransigencies of Israel juxtaposed against God's enduring love and forgiveness.

Judges 3: 12 – "And the children of Israel did evil again in the sight of the Lord: and the Lord strengthened Eglon the king of Moab against Israel, because they had done evil in the sight of the LORD."

As a consequence, Eglon smote Israel and ruled Israel for eighteen years. At that time God harkened to the pleas of Israel and sent them a deliverer, Ehud. Under the pretext of sending Eglon a gift, Israel sent Ehud to the king.

Judges 3: 17 – "And he brought the present unto Eglon king of Moab, …"

Judges 3: 21 – "And Ehud put forth his left hand, and took the dagger from his right thigh, and thrust it into his belly:

Then Ehud flees to the mountain of Ephraim.

Judges 3: 27 – "And it came to pass, when he was come, that he blew a <u>trumpet</u> in the mountain of Ephraim, and the children of Israel went down with him from the mount, and he before them."

<u>*Judge 3: 28-30*</u>

Judges 3: 28 - "And he said unto them, Follow after me: for the Lord hath delivered your enemies the Moabites into your hand. And they went down after him, and took the fords of Jordan toward Moab, and suffered not a man to pass over."

Judges3: 29 – "And they slew of Moab at that time about ten thousand men, all lusty, and all men of valor; and their escaped not a man."

Judges3: 30 – "So Moab was subdued that day under the hand of Israel. And the land had rest fourscore years."

The stories of the military battle and the spiritual turmoil inexorably intertwine in the defeat of King Moab. To Israel the military victory was all-important, not so much the spiritual one, at least not important enough to prevent Israel from doing evil again in the sight of the Lord.

(sta) 26. - Trumpets played a significant role in the battle of Moab, a battle of both military and spiritual importance.

And so ends Chapter Seven

Chapter seven yields one significant trumpet association:

(sta) 26. – Trumpets played a significant role in the battle of Moab, a battle of both military and spiritual importance.

Notes and Reflections

Chapter Eight

Significant trumpet associations derived from the book of Judges.

The following verses tell the story of Israel's struggles against the Midianites; another struggle against another oppressor, and once again made necessary by Israel's failure to heed God's commandments.

The Midianites were a tribe of nomadic herdsman, descended from Midian, a son of the patriarch Abraham by his concubine Keturah.

Judges 6: 1 – "And the children of Israel did evil in the sight of the Lord: and the Lord delivered them into the hand of Midian seven years."

Due to their transgressions, (idol worship of the false gods Baal and Ashkerah) God handed Israel over to an oppressor.

But once more, God has mercy on his people Israel.

Judges 6: 7 – "And it came to pass, when the children of Israel cried unto the Lord because of the Midianites,"

Judges 6: 8 – "That the Lord sent a prophet unto the children of Israel …",

As a result of Israel's pleas for help, God sends an angel to visit Gideon the son of Joash the Abiezrite, and gives him instructions on how to defeat the Midianites.

Judges 6: 34 – "But the spirit of the Lord came upon Gideon, and he blew a <u>trumpet</u>; and Abiezer was gathered after him." *

Previously the Holy Spirit had empowered Gideon, the son of Joash the Abiezrite, to take action whereby he had taken ten men with him and threw down the altar of the idol Baal whom his father Joash and the people had been worshiping. Filled with the Holy Spirit of God, Gideon then blew a trumpet, inspiring his father, their kin and others to gather to him in support of what he had done and what he was about to do.

(sta) 27. – Preparing to battle Israel's oppressors, the Midianites, Gideon blows a trumpet, calling on his family clan, the Abiezerites, to join the ranks of his army.

When the time comes for the climactic battle against the army of Midian, Gideon, in accordance with God's plan uses only three hundred men for the forthcoming contest.

Judges 7: 16 – "And he divided the three hundred men into three companies, and he put a trumpet in every man's hand, with empty pitchers, and lamps within the pitchers."

(sta) 28. – In accordance with God's seemingly peculiar battle plan, Gideon prepared his meager, three hundred-strong-army by arming them with only trumpets, jars, and torches.

As regards (sta) 28: To present-day observers, as well as to the ancient Israelites, it would appear to be a strange and seemingly inadequate choice of weapons with which to conduct armed conflict. And to pit hundreds against thousands only emphasizes the likelihood of defeat on the battlefield. Nevertheless Gideon remains steadfast in obedience to God's will.

(sta) 29. – To those willing to acknowledge the collateral, spiritual significance of the instruments chosen by God to facilitate the carrying out of his will, the sound of the trumpet, whether heard physically or perceived spiritually can serve to remind us of certain truths.

(sta) 30. - God expects full compliance with his commands regardless of any perceived inconsistency with human logic regarding their content or with his means of communicating them, whether by trumpets, or other chosen instruments.

(sta) 31. – God's choice of weapons for Israel against Midian (trumpets, jars, torches) teaches us that it is folly to pick and choose, to decide that some of God's commands are in error or illogical, or without merit and to conclude therefore that it is safe to ignore or disobey them.

In the battle against the Midianites, Gideon, with his 300 soldiers, armed with trumpets, jars, and torches, represents the best face of Israel; faithful to our God who created them and willing to face vastly superior numbers of soldiers. When God spoke, they had ears to hear; when God showed them the way, they had eyes to see, and when God promised, they believed like children.

Please dear God; help me to face life's battles with the kind of faith, hope, and certitude that Gideon and the three hundred carried into their darkest hour.

Judges 7: 18 – "When I blow with a trumpet, I and all that are with me, then blow ye the trumpets also on every side of all the camp, and say, The sword of the Lord and of Gideon."

Judges 7: 19 – "So Gideon, and the hundred men that were with him, came unto the outside of the camp in the beginning of the middle watch; and they had but newly set the watch: and they blew the trumpets, and brake the pitchers that were in their hands."

Judges 7: 20 – "And the three companies blew the trumpets, and brake the pitchers, and held the lamps in their left hands, and the trumpets in their right hands to blow withal: and they cried, The sword of the Lord, and of Gideon."

Judges 7: 22 – "And three hundred blew the trumpets, and the Lord set every man's sword against his fellow, even throughout all the host: and the host fled to Bethshittah in Zererath, and to the border of Abel-meholah, unto Tabbath."

At the battle of Midian, the eardrum-shattering sound of 300 glass pitchers breaking combined with the voices of 300 strong warriors shouting, "The sword of Gideon", preceded by 300 trumpets blaring so loudly so as to rattle the senses of the Midianites, induced fear and panic to such a degree that they fled in disarray, resulting once again in a God-given victory for Israel when pitted against an army of seemingly insurmountable superiority.

Primal fear of the death of the human body is highly understandable. But a more profound respect for the nature of death might engender an even greater fear, the fear that when we die, our spirit, the spirit God breathed into us at our inception (the unique spirit that creates us in the image and likeness of God) might have become unsuitable for companionship with God in his eternal kingdom.

This unsuitability can occur as the result of stubborn, repetitive and inappropriate expression of that two-edged sword called free will.

At death it is the spirit that returns to God. The body returns to the dust from whence it came, and the soul (meaning life) ceases to exist. *

* - Genesis 3: 19 – "In the sweat of thy face shalt thou eat bread, till thou return unto the ground; for out of it wast thou taken: for dust thou art, and unto dust shalt thou return."

* - Ecclesiastes 12: 7 – "Then shall the dust return to the earth as it was: and the spirit shall return unto God who gave it."

(sta) 32. - As proven in the battle of Midian, fear, in this case induced by trumpets, glass pitchers and loud voices, can be a more decisive factor than many thousands of conventional weapons.

(sta) 33. - Our battle on earth is choosing between good and evil, between physical and spiritual. God's battle is with the devil.

God will win his battle. But how about you and me, will we heed the messages of the trumpets and His other chosen instruments?

Let's cash in with the winning ticket: Be good; embrace spiritual values.

(sta) 34. - Trumpets played a significant role in the battle of Midian, a battle of both military and spiritual importance.

And so ends Chapter Eight.

Chapter eight yields eight significant trumpet associations:

(sta) 27. – Preparing to battle Israel's oppressors the Midianites, Gideon blows a trumpet, calling his clan the Abiezerites, to join the ranks of his army.

(sta) 28. – In accordance with God's seemingly peculiar battle plan, Gideon prepares his meager, three hundred-strong-army by arming them with only trumpets, jars, and torches

(sta) 29. – To those willing to acknowledge the collateral, spiritual significance of the instruments chosen by God to facilitate the carrying out of his will, the sound of the trumpet, whether heard physically or perceived spiritually can serve to remind us of certain truths.

(sta) 30. - God expects full compliance with his commands regardless of any perceived inconsistency with human logic

regarding their content or with his means of communicating them, whether by trumpets, or other chosen instruments.

(sta) 31. – God's choice of weapons for Israel against Midian (trumpets, jars, torches) teaches us that it is folly to pick and choose, to decide that some of God's commands are in error or illogical, or without merit and to conclude therefore that it is safe to ignore or disobey them.

(sta) 32. - As proven in the battle of Midian, fear can be a more decisive factor than many thousands of conventional weapons

(sta) 33. - Our battle on earth is choosing between good and evil, between physical and spiritual. God's battle is with the devil.

God will win his battle. But how about you and me, will we heed the messages of the trumpets and His other chosen instruments?

Let's cash in with the winning ticket: Be good; embrace spiritual values.

(sta) 34. - Trumpets played a significant role in the battle of Midian, a battle of both military and spiritual importance.

Notes and Reflections

Chapter Nine

Significant Trumpet Associations derived from the book of 1 Samuel

Under intense pressure from the people of Israel, their religious leader Samuel appoints Saul as the king of Israel. By insisting that a person should be their king instead of the Lord, the people have committed a grave sin. In the next several verses presented below, Samuel berates them for this, (recounting some of the wonderful acts of love and mercy the Lord had bestowed on them) and for their sins of idolatry, but nevertheless, Samuel continues to pray for Israel, reminding them that the Lord had made Israel his special people:

1 Samuel 12: 6 – "And Samuel said unto the people, It is the Lord that advanced Moses and Aaron, and that brought your fathers up out of the land of Egypt.

1 Samuel 12: 8 – "When Jacob was come into Egypt, and your fathers cried unto the Lord, then the Lord sent Moses and Aaron, which brought forth your fathers out of Egypt, and made them dwell in this place.

1 Samuel 12: 9 – "And when they forgat the Lord their God, he sold them into the hand of Sisera, captain of the host of

Hazor, and into the hand of the Philistines, and into the hand of the king of Moab, and they fought against them."

1 Samuel 12: 10 – "And they cried unto the Lord, and said, We have sinned, because we have forsaken the Lord, and have served Baalim and Ashtaroth: but now deliver us out of the hand of our enemies, and we will serve thee."'

1 Samuel 12: 11 – "And the Lord sent Jerubbaal, and Bedan, and Jephthah, and Samuel, and delivered you out of the hand of your enemies on every side, and ye dwelled safe."

1 Samuel 12: 12 – "And when ye saw that Nahash the king of the children of Ammon came against you, ye said unto me, Nay; but a king shall reign over us: when the Lord your God was your king."

1 Samuel 12: 13 – "Now therefore behold the king whom ye have chosen, and whom ye have desired! and behold, the Lord hath set a king over you."

1 Samuel 12: 14 – "If ye will fear the Lord, and serve Him, and obey His voice, and not rebel against the commandment of the Lord, then shall both ye and also the king that reigneth over you continue following the Lord your God."

1 Samuel 12: 24 – "Only fear the Lord, and serve him in truth with all our heart: for consider how great things he hath done for you."

Samuel was indeed a great religious leader of the Jews. God authorized him to speak in His name; that as long as the people obeyed God, whatever Samuel said or promised, God would see to its happening. Reading these verses, we are reminded how loving and forgiving God is, but we are also instructed regarding the severe consequences of idol worship and other sins against the Lord. It was true then and it is true now that, "God is good, but He is no fool"*, and perhaps more importantly, God, our Creator Father is not to be trifled with."**

Both quotations originally appeared in "Jesus Says", an earlier book by this author, published by Xulon press

* - page 420

** - page 374

After two years in office, King Saul went to war with the Philistines. He sent his son, Jonathan into battle, and Jonathan did admirably. He won an important battle at Geba.

1 Samuel 13: 3 – *"And Jonathan smote the garrison of the Philistines that was in Geba, and the Philistines heard of it. And Saul blew the* trumpet *throughout all the land, saying, Let the Hebrews hear."*

This sounding of the trumpet was a celebratory trump of Jonathan's victory, a warning of a larger threat yet to be dealt with, and a rallying cry. The Philistines fleeing from their defeat at Geba, and their main forces would mobilize against Saul's two thousand assembled at Micmash and Bethel.

(sta) 35. – Trumpet sounds were customized to convey their intended messages by varying the pitch and duration of fluctuating multiples of trumpets relayed from one outpost

to the next. *This tactic was instrumental in allowing Israel to achieve military victories beyond her numerical strength.*

And so ends Chapter Nine

Chapter nine yields one significant trumpet association:

(sta) 35. – – Trumpet sounds were customized to convey their intended messages by varying the pitch and duration of fluctuating multiples of trumpets relayed from one outpost to the next. This tactic was instrumental in allowing Israel to achieve military victories beyond her numerical strength.

Notes and Reflections

_____
_____
_____
_____
_____
_____
_____
_____
_____
_____
_____
_____
_____
_____
_____
_____
_____
_____
_____
_____
_____
_____
_____
_____
_____
_____
_____
_____

Chapter Ten

Significant trumpet associations derived from the book of 2 Samuel

Following Jonathan's victory over the Philistines at Geba, he and his father Saul lose their lives whilst doing battle with the Philistines at mount Giboah.

David, who will soon be anointed king of Judah, mourns their passing in a touching tribute as typified by the following four verses of his lament:

2 Samuel 1: 19, 23, 26, 27

1: 19 – "The beauty of Israel is slain upon thy high places: how are the mighty fallen!"

1: 23 – "Saul and Jonathan were lovely and pleasant in their lives, and in their death they were not divided: they were swifter than eagles, they were stronger than lions."

1: 26 – "I am distressed for thee, my brother Jonathan: very pleasant hast thou been unto me: thy love to me was wonderful, passing the love of women.

Francis J. Connelly

1: 27 –"How are the mighty fallen, and the weapons of war perished!"

At God's command David and his people go up to Hebron. It is there that the men of Judah anoint David as their king.

But this does not sit well with Abner the son of Ner, the captain of Saul's host.

Instead of accepting David as king, he designates Saul's son Ishbosheth as king over all Israel in opposition to David, the king of Judah.

Afterward an important battle takes place at Gibeon:

2 Samuel 2: 17 – "And there was a very sore battle that day; and Abner was beaten, and the men of Israel, before the servants of David."

<u>*2 Samuel 2: 25-28*</u>

2: 25 – "And the children of Benjamin gathered themselves together after Abner, and became one troop, and stood on the top of a hill.

2: 26 "Then Abner called to Joab, and said, Shall the sword devour forever: knowest thou not that it will be bitterness in the latter end?" how long shall it be then, ere thou bid the people return from following their brethren?

2: 27 – "And Joab said, As God liveth, unless thou hadst spoken, surely then in the morning the people had gone up every one from following his brother.

2: 28 – "So Joab blew a <u>trumpet</u>, and all the people stood still, and pursued after Israel no more, neither fought they any more.

(sta) 36. – Midst the hills of Ammah, in the wilderness of Gibeon, the trumpet sounds the end of a battle whilst there still remains a remnant of the foe available for pursuit and slaughter, a significant departure from the traditional aftermath of such an encounter. In this instance however the trumpet was significantly associated with the cause of peace and mercy.

(sta) 37 - The trumpet sound is the sound of heaven's will, whether they are blared in good times or bad, and whether or not they are instrumental in various stages of armed conflict, or (when at God's command more than three thousand years ago) they announced and celebrated that most important holyday The Feast Of trumpets, a day decreed by God to be a day of "holy convocation", a day of rest and a day wherein the blowing of trumpets is done as a memorial.

2 Samuel 6: 12 – "… So David went and brought up the ark of God * from the house of Obed-edom into the city of David with gladness."

* - The Ark of God, also known as The Ark of the Lord, The Ark of the Covenant, and The Ark of Testimony contained the two stone tablets upon which were written the Ten Commandments, the foundation of God's covenant with the people of Israel.

---

2 Samuel 6: 15 – "So David and all the house of Israel brought up the ark of the Lord with shouting, and with the sound of the <u>trumpet</u>."

2 Samuel 6: 16 - "And as the ark of the Lord came into the city of David, Michal, Saul's daughter looked through a window, and saw king David leaping and dancing before the Lord; and she despised him in her heart." *

* - Not only was Michal Saul's daughter, she was also the wife of David, so her vile response to David's celebration of God's glory served to reveal a heart filled with hatred for her husband David and for her creator God.

(sta) 38. – Sometimes, depending on who is observing and doing the listening, the trumpet sound can say, "Look at me, look at me, look at what I have done. I am dancing and leaping with joy because I am great" or it can say," Look, look at what God hath wrought. I am leaping and dancing with joy because our Lord our God is great."

<u>*2 Samuel 6: 21-23*</u>

"And David said unto Michael, it was before the Lord, which chose me before thy father, and therefore before all his house, to appoint me ruler over the people of the Lord, over Israel: therefore will I play before the Lord.

And I will yet be more vile than thus, and will be base in my own sight: and of the maidservants which thou hast spoken of, of them I shall I be had in honor.

Therefore Michal the daughter of Saul had no child unto the day of her death."

In accordance with the word of God, King David brought what was perhaps the most revered and important physical object of old testament days, The Ark of God to Jerusalem, the sacred city also referred to as the city of David.

In tribute to this sacred object, and with great shouts of happiness, trumpets blared, and David the king leaped and danced with abandon in appreciation of the great honor and responsibility with which God had entrusted him.

In response to Michal's criticisms, (sparked by her resentment of David's selection as king of Israel over her father Saul) David announced that the maidservants would be consorts of the king, but that Michal would never be, thereby condemning her to a lifetime without giving life.

* A cruel fate to inflict on a Hebrew woman.

(sta) 39. - The sound of trumpets can sometimes signal great joy and spiritual fervor. Those who are one with the Lord in obedience and love may rightfully join the party. Those who are not truly onboard, neither in faith nor in love and find ways to attack the righteously elated, often disguising their hate filled motives under the guise of moral indignation, are not invited.

(sta)40. – When the trumpet sound signals a time of great joy and spiritual fervor, those who attack the righteously elated do so at great peril to their physical and spiritual health.

2 Samuel 15: 10 – "But Absalom sent spies throughout all the tribes of Israel, saying, As soon as ye hear the sound of the <u>trumpet</u>, then ye shall say, Absalom reigneth in Hebron."

Absalom, son of David conspired to betray king David. His spies visited the tribes of Israel telling them that when the trumpet sounded, Absalom was king, thereby rallying the people to his cause. After all, it is more palatable to swear love and allegiance to a winner than it is to a loser. Based on the information provided by Absalom's spies many men of Israel did pledge to Absalom, but ultimately his treachery resulted in bitter consequences.

(sta) 41. – In ancient times, the trumpet is like a firearm, in that, when under the control of good men, it can be used for good purposes – (self defense, protection of the innocent, the conduct of just wars, etc.), whereas when under the control of treacherous men, the trumpet can be used to carry out nefarious schemes of deception such as envisioned by Absalom, and for other evil purposes.

Eventually a great battle took place between Israel, led by Absalom, against the army of king David, led by his three designated commanders: Joab, Abashi, and Ittai. Although Absalom's army greatly outnumbered king David's, his numerical superiority was negated by David's deployment of three armies attacking Absalom from three directions in a place called the wood of Ephraim.

<u>*2 Samuel 6-8*</u>

2 Samuel 6 - "So the people went out into the field against Israel; and the battle was in the wood of Ephraim;"

2 Samuel 7 - "Where the people of Israel were slain before the servants of David, and there was there a great slaughter that day of twenty thousand men."

2 Samuel 8 – "For the battle was there scattered over the face of all the county: and the wood devoured more people that day than the sword devoured."

At the end of the battle of the wood at Ephraim, Absalom became hopelessly entangled in the low-lying branches of a tree and it was there that Joab, despite king David's specific order not to kill his son Absalom, did kill Absalom.

2 Samuel 18: 16 – "And Jacob blew the <u>trumpet</u>, and the people returned from pursuing after Israel: for Joab held back the people."

Instead of showing mercy to Absalom in accordance with David's orders, Joab slew Absalom, and perversely, rather than pursuing the enemy army and slaughtering as many as possible, thereby greatly reducing the threat of subsequent battles by them against king David, he chose to hold back his men. However, it turned out that Joab's decisions were well calculated. Due to his counsel to David, diplomacy eventually ruled the day. David returned to Israel and Israel returned to David.

(sta) 42. - The trumpet blare can begin a war, or sound the peace.

2 Samuel 20: 1 – "And there happened to be there a man of Belial, whose name was Sheba, the son of Bichri, a Benjamite: and he blew a <u>trumpet</u>, and said, We have no *part in David, neither have we inheritance in the son of Jesse: every man to his tents, O Israel."*

The term, "a man of Belial" is used to identify a person as having little or no worth, or as godless, and it is sometimes used to designate a person as a demon or even as Satan himself. But in the case of 2 Samuel 20: 1 ^, the term most appropriately means, "rebel".

Belial was the son of Bichri, a Benjamite. The tribe of Benjamin was a northern tribe. The first king of Israel was Saul, a Benjamite. The Benjamites had supported Saul over David, an enduring tendency that was readily available to a rabble-rouser such as Sheba.

But let's take a look at whom the Israelites, led by Sheba were attempting to overthrow, - no less a personage than king David!

And as recorded in the gospel according to Luke we are informed that David is ancestor to Joseph the adoptive father of Jesus the Christ. Because of this ancestry Jesus was correctly called, "a son of David and therefore the rightful heir to the throne of David. Jesus was born in Bethlehem. Bethlehem is known as, "the city of David." *

* - Luke 2: 4 – "And Joseph also went up from Galilee, out of the city of Nazareth into Judea, unto the city of David, which is called Bethlehem; because he was of the house and lineage of David."

Most tellingly, the gospel according to Luke identifies the kingdom over which Jesus will reign forever as the spiritual offshoot of David's kingdom.

The angel Gabriel is sent by God to inform Mary of the incarnation of Jesus in her womb:

<u>*Luke 1: 30-33*</u> – *"And the angel said unto her, Fear not, Mary: for thou hast found favor with God.*

And behold, thou shalt conceive in thy womb, and bring forth a son, and shalt call his name Jesus.

He shall be called great, and shall be called the Son of the Highest: and the Lord God shall give unto him the throne of his father David:

And he shall reign over the house of Jacob for ever; and of his kingdom there shall be no end."

The story of Sheba, son of Bichri, a Benjamite should be a sobering tale to those drunk on the intoxicating wine of self-deception. Fueled by a bloated sense of self- esteem, accommodation to powerful carnal values can result in non-acceptance, or outright rejection of God's will, leading to the formulation of ideas and plans designed to thwart His intentions.

The odyssey of Sheba is a cautionary tale, the story of a rebel with a cause, but not a good one.

In order to emphasize the clear connection of cause to effect, 2 Samuel 20: 1 - (the cause) is re-presented below, followed by 2 Samuel 20: 22 – (the effect):

2 Samuel 20: 1 – *"And there happened to be there a man of Belial, whose name was Sheba, the son of Bichri, a Benjamite: and he blew a <u>trumpet</u>, and said, We have no* *part in David, neither have we inheritance in the son of Jesse: every man to his tents, O Israel."*

2 Samuel 20: 22 – "Then the woman went unto all the people in her wisdom. And they cut off the head of Sheba the son of Bichri, and cast it out to Joab. And he blew <u>a trumpet</u>, and they retired from the city, every man to his tent, And Joab returned to Jerusalem unto the king."

(sta) 43. - An initial trumpet sound can be the rallying signal that promises the fresh start of a new day, the imminent crowning of a more righteous king, or the establishment of a fairer government more sympathetic to the needs of the people.

(sta) 44. – Whatever the aspirations of the author of the initial trumpet sound and regardless of the methods employed to attain the goals promised, if the aspirations or the methods are in conflict with God's intentions, the final blare of the trumpet will serve as a death knell, (whether physical, and/or spiritual) of the initial promisor, and of his promises.

And so ends Chapter Ten

Chapter ten yields nine significant trumpet associations:

(sta) 36. – Midst the hills of Ammah, in the wilderness of Gibeon the trumpet sounds the end of a battle whilst there still remains a remnant of the foe available for pursuit and slaughter, a significant departure from the traditional aftermath of such an encounter. In this instance however the trumpet was significantly associated with the cause of peace and mercy.

(sta) 37 - The trumpet sound is the sound of heaven's will, whether they are blared in good times or bad, and whether or not they are instrumental in various stages of armed conflict, or (when at God's command more than three thousand years ago) they announced and celebrated that most important holyday The Feast Of trumpets, a day decreed by God to be a day of "holy convocation", a day of rest and a day wherein the blowing of trumpets is done as a memorial.

(sta) 38. – Sometimes, depending on who is observing and doing the listening, the trumpet sound can say, "Look at me, look at me, look at what I have done. I am dancing and leaping with joy because I am great" or it can say," Look, look at what God hath wrought. I am leaping and dancing with joy because our Lord our God is great."

(sta) 39. - The sound of trumpets can sometimes signal great joy and spiritual fervor. Those who are one with the Lord in obedience and love may rightfully join the party. Those who are not truly onboard, neither in faith nor in love and find ways to attack the righteously elated, often disguising their hate filled motives under the guise of moral indignation,

(sta) 40. – When the trumpet sound signals a time of great joy and spiritual fervor, those who attack the righteously elated do so at great peril to their physical and spiritual health.

(sta) 41. – In ancient times, the trumpet is like a firearm, in that, when under the control of good men, it can be used for good purposes – (self defense, protection of the innocent, the conduct of just wars, etc.), whereas when under the control of treacherous men, the trumpet can be used to carry out

nefarious schemes of deception such as envisioned by Absalom and for other evil purposes.

(sta) 42. - The trumpet blare can begin a war, or sound the peace.

(sta) 43. - An initial trumpet sound can be the rallying signal that promises the fresh start of a new day, the imminent crowning of a more righteous king, or the establishment of a fairer government more sympathetic to the needs of the people.

(sta) 44. – Whatever the aspirations of the author of the initial trumpet sound and regardless of the methods employed to attain the goals promised, if the aspirations or the methods are in conflict with God's intentions, the final blare of the trumpet will serve as a death knell, (whether physical, and/or spiritual) of the initial promisor, and of his promises.

Notes and Reflections

Chapter Eleven

A fervent prayer followed by additional commentary and excerpts of Scripture.

Please God let me be an instrument of peace and mercy in accordance with thy divine will. Give me the strength and courage to be a soldier of Christ in the face of a world gone mad with lust, hate, and pride. Let your will be done. Please come back quickly. We are not ready for your return, but it seems as though if you don't end this current age soon, the hate and self-pride, the selfishness and evil will continue to grow exponentially. Unless things change soon and dramatically, mankind will fail the intended purpose of your magnificent gift of free-will, a gift that, depending on how we use it, can either benefit us greatly, or condemn us even more greatly. We have the opportunity of choosing either God and spiritual values or Satan and worldly values.

As we go about our daily lives, there is a dramatic and powerful disconnect at work. One of the most potent manifestations of this disconnect is our understanding of time; the tendency of many to equate the two thousand years of its passage since Jesus last walked the earth with a corresponding diminution of the validity, truth, and redemptive power of His ministry wherein He preached a

Gospel of salvation for those who repent of their sins and accept Him as Lord and Savior.

Truth is an eternal factor, undiminished by time, unaltered by its passing. When Jesus walked the earth, He was the personification of truth. And when next He returns, this time in power and in glory, He will accomplish what has been promised in prophecy: Jesus will Rapture His Church, a church consisting of all believers who ever lived, past, present, and future; those who have gone to their rest in hope of rising again and those believers alive at the time. All will He raise to meet Him in the clouds of heaven with new and perfect spiritual bodies.

In his epistles to the churches at Thessalonica and Corinth, Paul speaks of these matters:

<u>*1 Thessalonians 4: 13-18*</u>

4: 13 - "But I would not have you to be ignorant, brethren, concerning them which are asleep, that ye sorrow not, even as others which have no hope.

4: 14 – "For if we believe that Jesus died and rose again, even so, Them also which sleep in Jesus will God bring with him".

4: 15 – "For this we say unto you by the word of the Lord, that we which are alive and remain unto the coming of the Lord shall not prevent them which are asleep."

4: 16 – "For the Lord himself shall descend from heaven with a shout, with the voice of the archangel

"4: 17 – "Then we which are alive, and remain shall be caught up together with them in the clouds to meet the Lord in the air; and so shall we ever be with the Lord."

4: 18 – "Wherefore comfort one another with these words.

1 Corinthians 15: 51-53

15: 51 - "Behold, I show you a mystery; We shall not all sleep, but we shall all be changed."

15:52 – "In a moment, in the twinkling of an eye, at the last trump: for the <u>trumpet</u> shall sound, and the dead shall be raised incorruptible, and we shall be changed.

15: 53 – "For this corruptible must put on incorruption, and this mortal must put on immortality. *

* - The spirits of those who have died in Christ will be resurrected with incorruptible bodies, bodies not subject to illness and death, spiritual bodies no longer susceptible to the ravages of carnal and worldly impulses.

(sta) 45. – When next Jesus comes again, the trumpet sound will signal the initiation of the transformation from corruptible physical bodies to incorruptible spiritual ones, both for the living, and for the dead in Christ.

And they too, those who are alive at the time of the Rapture will be transformed, blessed with new and perfect spiritual bodies.

At the Rapture, all those who have died believing in Jesus will be resurrected with new and wonderful bodies and will meet Jesus in the clouds. All the believers alive at that time will join the resurrected with new and wonderful bodies, and together they will join Jesus in heaven.

In death, time is no factor, ergo those raised from the dead will not have experienced nor been cognizant of the passage of time.

When a person dies –(gone to his rest in the hope of rising again) it is his spirit that returns to God's safekeeping; the body returns to the dust from whence it came, nevermore to exist. It is the spirit of a man that speaks of who he is and what he is. It is the spirit that is judged; it is the spirit that is immortal; it is the spirit of a man that defines him, not his body, not his mind, and not his soul:

Ecclesiastes 12: 7 – "Then shall the dust return to the earth as it was: and the spirit shall return unto God who gave it."

Genesis 3: 19 – "In the sweat of thy face shalt thou eat bread, till thou return unto the ground; for out of it wast thou taken: for dust thou art, and unto dust shalt thou return."

And it is to the spirit, and of spiritual things that Jesus concerned Himself with during His three years ministry on earth. Recognition and acceptance of this factor can go a long way in allowing non-believers to overcome doubts fueled by what they perceive as justified obstacles to their full acceptance of the Gospels. For example, when Pilate asked Jesus why, if Jesus was a king, did He not call on His army to rescue Him from his current peril, the simple logic of Jesus' reply left Pilate somewhat dumbfounded –("My kingdom is not of this world: …") - John 18: 36

Additional evidence of the claim that spiritual reality is the basis for Jesus' teachings can be found in the gospel according to John:

The Chief rabbi, and the other temple leaders had complained to Pontius Pilate that Jesus claimed to be a king. If this proved to be true, Jesus would be guilty of treason against the Roman Empire, a crime punishable by death. During His three years ministry, Jesus had preached the gospel of repentance leading to salvation and citizenship in God's coming kingdom. As a result of the accusations of the Jews, Jesus is led to the hall of judgment where Pontius Pilate questions him:

John – 18: 33-38

"*… Art thou the King of the Jews?*

Jesus answered him,

"*Sayest thou this thing of thyself, or did others tell it thee of me?*

"*Pilate answered, Am I a Jew? Thine own nation and the chief priests have delivered thee unto me: what hast thou done?*

Jesus answered,

My kingdom is not of this world: if my kingdom were of this world, then would my servants fight, that I should not be delivered to the Jews: but now is my kingdom not from hence.

"*Pilate therefore said unto him, Art thou a king then? Jesus answered,*"

Thou sayest that I am a king. To this end was I born, and for this cause came I into the world, that I should bear witness unto the truth. Every one that is of the truth heareth my voice.)

Another example supporting the idea that spiritual reality is the basis for Jesus' teachings can be found in Paul's first letter to the Corinthians:

It contains what is reputedly, the earliest written account of the 'Last Supper':

1 Corinthians 11: 23-26

"For I have received of the Lord that which also I delivered unto you, That the Lord Jesus the same night in which he was betrayed took bread:

And when he had given thanks, he brake it, and said, Take, eat: this is my body which is broken for you: this do in remembrance of me.

After the same manner also he took the cup, when he had supped, saying, This cup is the new testament in my blood: this do ye, as oft as ye drink it, in remembrance of me. For as often as ye eat this bread, and drink this cup, ye do show the Lord's death till he come."

The Bread is the spiritual body of Jesus, which He gave up for us on the cross of Golgotha. When we give thanks and eat bread in remembrance of Him, we partake of Jesus' spiritual body; we are spiritually nourished, and we reaffirm and strengthen our inclusion as members of the church instituted by Jesus.

The cup of wine is the spiritual blood of Jesus shed at the crucifixion. When we give thanks and drink wine in remembrance of Him, we reaffirm our belief and membership in The New Testament, a testament of salvation foretold by prophets, paid for by crucifixion, and fulfilled by Jesus' resurrection and ascension into heaven, taking His rightful place at the right hand of the Father.

In the gospel according to John it is recorded that Jesus tells us:

"It is the spirit that quickeneth; the flesh profiteth nothing: the words that I speak unto you, they are spirit, and they are life." – John 6: 63.

* - "Quickeneth" means, gives life to. "Spirit" means, that which comes from God.

All of Jesus' teachings, including the above verses dealing with the bread and the wine as they relate to Jesus' flesh and blood are best understood when viewed thru a prism of spiritual reality.

At this point, "A Fervent prayer followed by additional commentary and excerpts of Scripture" ends. The specific text of "Softly Now The Trumpet" continues.

And so ends Chapter Eleven.

Chapter eleven yields one significant trumpet association:

(sta) 45. – When next Jesus comes again, the trumpet sound will signal the initiation of the transformation from corruptible physical bodies to incorruptible spiritual ones, both for the living, and for the dead in Christ.

Notes and Reflections

Chapter Twelve

Significant trumpet associations derived from the book of 1 Kings.

In the waning years of King David's reign, he had become old and feeble, neither strong of body nor intellectually robust. In an attempt to rouse his spirits, generate physical heat and to possibly spike the king's mental acuity, his servants took bold, and what they hoped would be, remedial steps:

First they clothed David with warm clothes, and on top of them they piled skins and furs intended to contain body heat, but as scripture tells us,

"he gat no heat." - 1 Kings 1: 1

I Kings 1: 2 – "Wherefore his servants said unto him, Let there be sought for my lord the king a young virgin: and let her stand before the king, and let her cherish him, and let her lie in thy bosom, that my lord the king may get heat."

So throughout the land a search went out to find the fairest of the fair. And behold,

Abishag a Shunammite was found and brought to the king.

* - (Author's note) - One might be tempted to comment, "It's good to be king", but King David was unable to react satisfactorily to the good intentions of his servants:

1 Kings 1: 4 – "And the damsel was very fair, and cherished the king, and ministered to him: but the king knew her not."

Although the preceding two verses and commentary are not directly related to trumpets, they are included here to emphasize the advanced years of king David and his reliance on loyal followers at a time when more serious matters (matters that involve the use of trumpets) are about to come into play.

And as the following verses allude to, the price to be paid as a consequence of the ravages of old age can be more potentially consequential than the diminution of body-heat.

Adonijah, a son of David, (mother-Haggith) favored by David, second only to Absalom, attempts to wrest the throne away from David before the king's demise.

Two important personages assist Adonijah, Joab the captain of the army and Abiathar the priest. Together they proclaimed Adonijah as the new king of Israel:

1 Kings 1: 5 –"Then Adinojah the son of Haggith exalted himself, saying, I will be king: and he prepared him chariots and horsemen, and fifty men to run before him."

I Kings 1: 7 – "And he conferred with Joab the son of Zeruiah, and with Abiathar the priest: and they following Adonijah helped him.

But Adonijah failed to gain the support of Zadok the priest, Benaiah the commander of the royal bodyguard, or Nathan the prophet. Acting in concert with Bathsheba, these three manage to convince David of Adonijah's perfidy, whereupon David arranges to proclaim his son Solomon (divinely ordained to inherit the kingship) as the new king of Israel and Judah:

(sta) 46. - No trumpet sound accompanied Adonijah's failed attempt to become king.

Unless it is within the realm of God's will, no trumpet lends credence to a coronation.

David the king commands:

1 Kings 1: 34 - "And let Zadok the priest and Nathan the prophet anoint him their king over Israel: and blow ye with the trumpet, and say, God save king Solomon."

(sta) 47 - – The trumpet's blare may pronounce the accomplishment of God's will, and/or celebrate the inspired recognition of His will be done.

And in perfect obedience, Zadok the priest anoints Solomon with oil from the tabernacle, Nathan the prophet, by his presence attests to the prophetic rectitude of the anointing, and Benaiah the commander of the royal bodyguard causes the trumpet to sound:

1 Kings 1: 39 - "And Zadok the priest took a horn of oil out of the tabernacle, and anointed Solomon. And they blew the <u>trumpet</u>; and all the people said, God save King Solomon."

A thousand years afterward, as recorded in the gospel according to Matthew, Chapter 1, verses 6-17, (not repeated here) the genealogy of Jesus of Nazareth is stated wherein it is proclaimed that Jesus is descended from King David and is therefore qualified to be referred to as a son David.

And in the gospel according to Luke it is recorded that the angel Gabriel is sent by God to inform Mary of the incarnation of Jesus in her womb, and that he would be recognized as a son of David:

<u>Luke 1: 30-33</u> – "And the angel said unto her, Fear not, Mary: for thou hast found favor with God.

And behold, thou shalt conceive in thy womb, and bring forth a son, and shalt call his name Jesus.

He shall be called great, and shall be called the Son of the Highest: and the Lord God shall give unto him <u>the throne of his father David</u>:

And he shall reign over the house of Jacob for ever; and of his kingdom there shall be no end."

Had David not overturned and delegitimized Adonijah's rebellious elevation to kingship, the genealogy of Jesus would not have developed along the bloodlines in accordance with God's wishes. But of course, 'God's will, will be done', then, now, and always.

(sta) 48 - When the trumpet serves God's purpose, its sound is heavenly, whether celebratory or congratulatory, or when solemn-sad or happily glad and all the steps between. Then it is heaven sent, God's chosen instrument.

After the lawful succession of Solomon to the throne of king David, there was much celebration:

<u>*1 Kings 1: 39-41*</u> *- "And Zadok the priest took a horn of oil out of the tabernacle and anointed Solomon. And they blew the <u>trumpet</u>; and all the people said, God save king Solomon.*

And all the people came up after him, and the people piped with pipes, and rejoiced with great joy, so that the earth rent with the sound of them.

And Adonijah and all the guests that were with him heard it as they made an end of eating. And when Joab heard the sound of the <u>trumpet</u>, he said, Wherefore is this noise of the city being in an uproar?"

The uproar, of course was the celebration of Solomon being crowned king after David.

And even though Adonijah had sought to wrongfully become king over Solomon, Solomon forgave him:

<u>*1 Kings 1: 51-53*</u> *– And it was told Solomon, saying, Behold, Adonijah feareth king Solomon: for, lo, he hath caught hold on the horns* of the altar, saying, Let king Solomon swear unto me this today that he will not slay his servant with the sword.*

And Solomon said, If he will show himself a worthy man, there shall not be a hair of him fall to the earth: but if wickedness shall be found in him, he shall die.

So king Solomon sent, and they brought him down from the altar. And he came and bowed himself to king Solomon: and Solomon said unto him, Go to thine house." **

* - Attached to the four corners of the altar in the temple and in the tabernacle were four horns. Adinojah grasped the horns and held on for dear life as he pleaded his case, hoping that no harm would come to him in such a holy place.

** - "Go to thine house" were words like music to the ears of Adinojah. To be free to return to his own house meant freedom from fear of righteous retribution by king David, freedom to conduct daily affairs sans official sanctions, and freedom to either pursue the straight and narrow path of obedience to the rightful king, David, or to follow the back roads of treachery and deceit which would hopefully lead to another shot at the golden crown of kingship.

After David had passed away, Adonijah, once again by devious means, attempts to be proclaimed king. As a result of Adonijah"s continued intransigence, king Solomon orders that Adonijah be killed:

<u>*1 Kings 2: 24-25*</u> - *"Now therefore, as the Lord liveth, which hath established me on the throne of my father David, and who hath made me a house, as he promised,*

Adonijah shall be put to death this day.

And king Solomon sent by the hand of Benaiah the son of Jehoiada; and he fell upon him that he died."

Some people never learn. Some people are so blinded by raw, naked ambition and so deafened by the roar of power-lust that they can neither see the plain truth, nor hear words of wisdom. Nothing, short of death, can put an end to their relentless pursuit of carnal ambitions.

So ends Chapter Twelve.

Chapter twelve yields three significant trumpet associations:

(sta) 46. - No trumpet sound accompanied Adonijah's failed attempt to become king.

Unless it is within the realm of God's will, no trumpet lends credence to a coronation.

(sta) 47 - – The trumpet's blare may pronounce the accomplishment of God's will, and/or celebrate the inspired recognition of His will be done.

(sta) 48 - When the trumpet serves God's purpose, its sound is heavenly, whether celebratory or congratulatory, or when solemn-sad or happily glad and all the steps between. Then it is heaven sent, God's chosen instrument.

Notes and Reflections

Chapter Thirteen

Significant trumpet associations derived from the book of 2 Kings:

A servant of Elisha, in obedience to that prophet's instructions, pours oil on the head of Jehu a captain of the host of Ahab, reciting the words he had been instructed to say:

2 Kings 9: 6 – "…. Thus saith the Lord God of Israel, "I have anointed thee king over the people of the Lord, even over Israel."

The other captains of Ahab's host immediately recognize the legitimacy of Jehu's elevation to the kingship of Israel, accepting the divine authority from which it derived:

2 Kings 9:13 - "Then they hasted, and took every man his garment, and put it under him on the top of the stairs, and blew the trumpets, saying, Jehu is king."

(sta) 49. – The trumpet's blare may pronounce the accomplishment of God's will, and/or celebrate the inspired recognition of His will be done.

When Athaliah, the mother of the dead king Ahaziah learned of Ahaziah's death (a death sanctioned by God) she attempted to do away with all the royal seed – (the (legitimate heirs to the throne of Ahaziah). In that way she would be able to rule as Queen. And she did so for six years. But Jehosheba the sister of Ahaziah, with the help of the chief priest Jehoiada eventually thwarted her plans. She had hid Joash, the son of the late king in her quarters for six years.

In the seventh year of Athaliah's reign, Jehoiada the chief priest made a covenant with the captains of the Carites - (the elite royal bodyguards), swearing them under oath in the house of the Lord. Thereby the final stage of the plan was formulated and the trap set to dethrone Queen Athaliah:

<u>*2 Kings 11: 11-20*</u>

11: 11 - "And the guards stood, every man with his weapons in his hands, from the south side of the house to the north side of the house, around the altar and the house on behalf of the king."

11: 12 – "Then he brought out the king's son and put the crown on him and gave the testimony. And they proclaimed him king and anointed him, and they clapped their hands and said, "Long live the king!"

11: 13 – "And when Athaliah heard the noise of the guard and of the people, she came to the people into the temple of the Lord."

11: 14 – "And when she looked, behold, the king stood by a pillar, as the manner was, and the princes, and the <u>trumpeters</u> by the king, and all the people of the land rejoiced, and blew with <u>trumpets:</u> and Athaliah rent her clothes, and cried, Treason, treason."

11: 15 – "But Jehoiada the priest commanded the captains of the hundreds, the officers of the host, and said unto them,

Have her forth without the ranges: and him that followeth her kill with the sword. For the priest had said, Let her not be slain in the house of the Lord."

11: 16 – "And they laid hands on her; and she went by the way by the which the horses came into the king's house: and there was she slain."

11: 17 – "And Jehoiada made a covenant between the Lord and the king and the people, that they should be the Lord's people; between the king also and the people."

11: 18 – "And all the people of the land went into the house of Baal, and brake it down; his altars and his images brake they in pieces thoroughly, and slew Mattan the priest of Baal before the altars. And the priest appointed officers over the house of the Lord."

11: 19 – "And he took the rulers over hundreds and the captains, and the guard, and all the people of the land; and they brought down the king from the house of the Lord, and came by the way of the gate of the guard to the king's house. And he sat on the throne of the kings."

11: 20 – "And all the people of the land rejoiced and the city was in quiet: and they slew Athaliah with the sword beside the king's house."

11: 21 – "Seven years old was Jehoash when he began to reign,"

(sta) 50. - Depending on which side of life's equation one inhabits, either the carnal -(lover and seeker of worldly values), or the spiritual –(lover and seeker of spiritual values), the mere presence of lawfully authorized trumpeters can strike fear, or engender joy.

Schemers scheme, often with apparent good success, but the question is how do you measure success? For almost seven years Athaliah reigned as queen, even though she committed murder to do so. For six years Jehosheba, with great peril to herself, hid and protected Joash, the rightful heir to the throne of her brother

Ahaziah. Her motive for doing so and the motive of the high priest who helped her was simply to do the right thing; to place the crown of kingship on the person chosen by God to wear it.

For a while (six years) carnal appetite and evil intention prevailed, but only for a while. Even if the evil queen had not been dethroned, but instead lived a long life as queen, judgment day would someday have come for her, as it will for all of us.

Schemers scheme (enthralled by worldly values and transient rewards), and dreamers dream (perhaps of self improvement, but absent the commensurate effort needed), but believers strive to live in accordance with God's will.

It is far better to be judged as a person who tried to do the right thing, rather than as a dreamer who dreamed his life away, or worse yet, as a schemer.

(sta) 51. - Divinely authorized trumpeters sounding God's chosen instruments can designate specifically targeted recipients as Schemers, Dreamers, or Believers.

2 Kings 12: 2 – "And Jehoash did that which was right in the sight of the Lord all his days wherein Jehoiada the priest instructed him.

2 Kings 12: 3 – "But the high places were not taken away: the people still sacrificed and burnt incense in the high places."

Although Jehoash was the chosen king, reigning in Jerusalem for a long period of time - (40yrs.), and was obedient to the will of God as advised by the high priest, there persisted a weakness in his administration in that, the 'high places'* were increasingly used to celebrate the holy days and perform the sacred rituals. The temple proper had been neglected. It was in need of repairs, both structurally and aesthetically.

* - "The high places" were originally physically high public spaces deemed suitable for congregational worship, but eventually the requirement that they be high physically was abandoned. The increased use of 'high places' to conduct religious rites, rather than devotions conducted in the temple contributed to a sense of diminution of the people's religious life.

An additional problem had further contributed to the structural, spiritual and aesthetical denigration of the temple. Apparently, not an adequate percentage of all the moneys coming into the temple were properly allocated for repairs and beautification. Consequently the king gave the following orders:

2 Kings 12: 4,5 – *"And Jehoash said to the priests, All the money of the dedicated things that is brought into the house of the Lord, even the money of every one that passeth the account, the money that every man is set at, and all the money that cometh into any man's heart to bring into the house of the Lord,*

Let the priests take it to them, every man of his acquaintance: and let them repair the breaches of the house, wheresoever any breach shall be found."

After a generous amount of time had passed since issuing his orders regarding physical repairs of the temple, the king realized that no progress had been made. He therefore ordered that the priests would no longer distribute temple moneys to friends and acquaintances for the purpose of temple upkeep. Instead, all moneys coming into the temple were collected at the door and deposited in a great chest.

Soon goodly amounts of money accumulated, enough so that the carpenters, builders, masons, hewers of stone were paid ample funds to repair the breaches of the temple.

Problem solved? No, not really:

2 Kings 12: 13,14 – *"Howbeit there were not made for the house of the Lord bowls of silver, snuffers, basins, trumpets, any vessels of gold or vessels of silver, of the money that was brought into the house of the Lord.*

But they gave that to the workmen, and repaired therewith the house of the Lord."

(sta) 52. – In order to comply fully with God's intentions regarding temple worship and rituals, it is necessary that certain sacred objects including trumpets be on hand and at the ready.

Although the physical condition of the temple continued to receive tender, loving care, the sacred objects necessary for the proper carrying out of divinely mandated practices and religious rituals were lacking.

We do not know the whole story of king Jehoash, but we do know enough, as the following verses and commentary will attest to, that his failure to provide the sacred objects, (bowls of silver, snuffers, basins, trumpets, and vessels of silver or vessels of gold) necessary for the proper function of the temple redounded to his extreme disadvantage:

2 Kings 12: 17, 18 – *"Then Hazael king of Syria went up and fought against Gath, and took it: and Hazael set his face to go up to Jerusalem.*

And Jehoash king of Judah took all the hallowed things that Jehoshaphat, and Jehoram, and Ahaziah, his father's, kings of Judah, had dedicated, and his own hallowed things, and all the gold that was found in the treasures of the house of the

Lord, and in the king's house, and sent it to Hazael king of Syria: and he went away from Jerusalem."

Not only did king Jehoash give to king Hazael the physical wealth of Jerusalem, he also turned over to him all the hallowed things of his forbearer kings and his own personal hallowed objects.

King Jehoash's over-the-top capitulation provided the means by which king Hazael was able to pillage Jerusalem of its objects of physical and spiritual wealth.

King Hazael got what he wanted and more, and as we learned in 2 Kings 12: 18, "he went away from Jerusalem."

The "extreme disadvantage" redounding to king Jahoash referred to earlier plays itself out shortly following the pauperization of Jerusalem's house of the Lord:

2 Kings 12: 20 – "And his servants arose, and made a conspiracy, and slew Joash in the house of Millo, …" *

* - The names Joash and Jehoash are considered interchangeable.

And so ends Chapter Thirteen.

Chapter thirteen yields four significant trumpet associations:

(sta) 49. – The trumpet's blare may pronounce the accomplishment of God's will, and/or celebrate the inspired recognition of His will be done.

(sta) 50. - Depending on which side of life's equation one inhabits, either the carnal -(lover and seeker of worldly values), or the spiritual –(lover and seeker of spiritual values), the mere presence of lawfully authorized trumpeters can strike fear, or engender joy.

(sta) 51. - Divinely authorized trumpeters sounding God's chosen instruments can designate specifically targeted recipients as Schemers, Dreamers, or Believers.

(sta) 52. – In order to comply fully with God's intentions regarding temple worship and rituals, it is necessary that certain sacred objects, including trumpets be on hand and at the ready.

Notes and Reflections

Chapter Fourteen

Significant trumpet associations derived from the book of

1 Chronicles

The two books of Chronicles (1 Chronicles and 2 Chronicles) provide details and additional information regarding the history of Israel not fully covered in 1 and 2 Samuel and 1 and 2 Kings. The information provided in Chronicles includes the religious institutions and practices that prevailed during that period and the lives of Israel's kings, particularly that of her greatest king, David.

1 Chronicles, chapter 13 records David's initial attempt to move The Ark of God to the royal city of Jerusalem.

At Davis' command, Ahio and Uzza moved the Ark out of the house of Abinadab with the goal of bringing it to Jerusalem, prompting David to celebrate:

1 Chronicles 13: 8 – "And David and all Israel played before God with all their might, and with singing, and with harps, and with psalteries, and with timbrels, and with cymbals, and with trumpets."

But as we learn from 1 Chronicles 13: 9, 10, disaster shortly comes to Uzza:

"And when they came unto the threshing floor of Chidon, Uzza put forth his hand to hold the ark; for the oxen had stumbled.

And the anger of the Lord was kindled against Uzza, and he smote him, because he put his hand to the ark: and there he died before Good."

And as things turned out, David's celebration was doubly premature and inappropriate because in his desire and haste to bring the Ark to Jerusalem, he had failed to properly prepare for the move.

Because of God's demonstrated displeasure with David's attempt to move the Ark to Jerusalem, David instead brought it into the house of Obed-edom the Gittite for a period of three months.

1 Chronicles 13: 14 – "And the ark of God remained with the family of Obed-edom in his house three months. And the lord blessed the house of Obed-edom, and all that he had." *

* - The inference here is that the mere presence of the Ark (and/or the safekeeping of it) brought forth divine blessings, perhaps of both material and spiritual value.

On the other hand though, it is well to remember that absent the power of the Holy Spirit, - (i.e., God) no person, place or thing is capable of bestowing divine blessings.

The shortcomings of this, David's first attempt at moving The Ark of the Covenant are revealed in 1 Chronicles, chapters 15 and 16 wherein David complies with law and precedent regarding moving the Ark, thereby succeeding in bringing it to Jerusalem. – (Appropriate Chapters and verses to follow.)

<u>*1 Chronicles 15: 1-3*</u>

"And David made him houses in the city of David, and prepared a place for the Ark of God, and pitched for it a tent.

Then David said, None ought to carry the ark of God but the Levites; for them hath the Lord chosen to carry the ark of God, and to minister unto him for ever.

15: 24 – "And Shebaniah, and Jehoshaphat, and Nethaneel, and Amasai, and Zechariah, and Benaiah, and Eliezer, the priests, did blow with the <u>trumpets</u> before the ark of God: and Obed-edom and Jehiah were doorkeepers for the ark."

15: 28 – "Thus all Israel brought up the ark of the covenant of the Lord with shouting, and with sound of the cornet, and with <u>trumpets</u>, and with cymbals, making a noise with psalteries and harps."

16: 6 – "Benaiah also and Jahaziel the priests with <u>trumpets</u> continually before the ark of the covenant of God."

16: 42 – "And with them Heman and Jeduthun with <u>trumpets</u> and cymbals for those that should make a sound, and with musical instruments of God. And the sons of Jeduthun were porters."

(sta) 53. – Joyful sounding trumpets may blare, but even if initiated at the behest of the greatest of earthly kings, without God's sanction they portend sad consequences.

(sta) 54. – Joyful trumpets may blare, and even if sounded at the behest of the least of us, with God's sanction they portend good news.

The Song of the Lord is recorded in 1 Chronicles 16: 8-36. It is a prayer to invoke, to thank, and to praise the Lord God of Israel. It is king David's prayer of thanks.

Even this - (Heaven on Earth), a most modest commentary of the Bible, featuring as it does, only one of the myriad intriguing aspects of the Good Book, i.e., the significant role played by trumpets, would benefit from providing the reader with an immediately available presentation of the prayer known as The Song of The Lord:

1 Chronicles 16: 8-36

"Give thanks unto the Lord, call upon his name, make known his deeds among the people.

Sing unto him, sing psalms unto him, talk ye of all his wondrous works.

Glory ye in his holy name: let the heart of them rejoice that seek the Lord.

Seek the Lord and his strength, seek his face continually.

Remember his marvelous works that he hath one. His wonders, and the judgments of his mouth;

O ye seed of Israel his servant, ye children of Jacob, his chosen ones.

He is the Lord our God; his judgments are in all the earth.

Be ye mindful always of his covenant; the word which he commanded to a thousand generations.

Even of the covenant which he made with Abraham, and of his oath unto Isaac.

And hath confirmed the same to Jacob for a law, and to Israel for an everlasting covenant,

Saying, Unto thee will I give the land of Canaan, the lot of your inheritance;

When ye were but a few, even a few, and strangers in it,

And when they went from nation to nation, and from one kingdom to another people;

He suffered no man to do them wrong: yea he reproved kings fore their sakes,

Saying, Touch not my appointed, and do my prophets no harm.

Sing unto the Lord, all the earth; show forth from day to day his salvation.

Declare his glory among the brethren; his marvelous works among all nations.

For great is the Lord, and greatly to be praised: he also is to be feared above all gods.

For all the gods of the people are idols: but the Lord made the heavens.

Glory and; honor are in his presence; strength and gladness are in his place.

Give unto the Lord, ye kindreds of the people, give unto the Lord glory and strength.

Give unto the Lord the glory due unto his name: bring an offering, and come before him: worship the Lord in the beauty of holiness.

Fear before him, all the earth: the world also shall be stabile, that it be not moved.

Let the heavens be glad, and let the earth rejoice: and let men say among the nations, The Lord reigneth.

Let the sea roar, and the fullness thereof: let the fields rejoice, and all that is therein.

Then shall the trees of the wood sing out at the presence of the Lord, because he cometh to judge the earth.

O give thanks unto the Lord; for he is good; for his mercy endureth for ever.

And say ye, Save us, O God of our salvation, and gather us together, and deliver us from the heathen, that we may give thanks to thy holy name, and glory in thy praise.

Blessed be the Lord God of Israel for ever and ever. And all the people said, A'-men, and praised the Lord."

And so ends Chapter Fourteen.

Chapter fourteen yields two significant trumpet associations:

(sta) 53. – Joyful sounding trumpets may blare, but even if initiated at the behest of the greatest of earthly kings, without God's sanction they portend sad consequences.

(sta) 54. – Joyful trumpets may blare and even if sounded at the behest of the least of us, with God's sanction they portend good news.

Notes and Reflections

_____

_____

_____

_____

_____

_____

_____

_____

_____

_____

_____

_____

_____

_____

_____

_____

_____

_____

_____

_____

_____

_____

_____

_____

_____

_____

_____

_____

_____

_____

_____

Chapter Fifteen

Significant trumpet associations derived from the book of 2 Chronicles:

Originally written as one book, the Chronicles record important aspect of Israel's history from the time of Adam until the fall of Jerusalem.

1 Chronicles ends with the death of David the king:

"And he died in a good old age, full of days, riches, and honor: and Solomon his son reigned in his stead." - 1 Chronicles 29: 28

2 Chronicles takes up the story of the time and times of Israel's kings starting with David's successor Solomon until the fall of Jerusalem in 586 B.C.

Orchestrated by Solomon, The Ark of God is brought into the Temple of the Lord:

2 Chronicles 5: 12 – "Also the Levites which were the singers, all of them of Asaph, of Heman, of Jeduthun, with their sons and their brethren, being arrayed in white linen, having cymbals and psalteries, and harps, stood at the east end of the *altar, and with them a hundred and twenty priests sounding with trumpets."**

* - Asaph, Heman, and Jeduthun, the descendants of the chief musicians were united, making music to glorify God.

(sta) 55. – Celebrating the installation of the Ark of God at Jerusalem, Israel experienced one of her finest moments:

She adhered to tradition, i.e., properly clad singers, duly authorized via custom and heritage, with their sons and brethren furnished with cymbals, psalteries, and harps, led by 120 priests playing the trumpets, united, one and all, worshiping the one true God, the God of Abraham, Isaac, and Jacob.

2 Chronicles 5: 13 – "It came even to pass, as the trumpeters and singers were as one, to make one sound to be heard in praising and thanking the Lord; and when they lifted up their voice with the trumpets and cymbals and instruments of music, and praised the Lord, saying, For he is good; for his mercy endureth for ever: that then the house was filled with a cloud, even the house of the Lord;"

(sta) 56. – Celebrating the installation of the Ark of God at Jerusalem, the trumpeters and singers blended their sounds in a manner so as to create one voice, possibly constituting the first one-sound combination of trumpet/voice in praise and glory of God.

Despite the absolute propriety of the goings-on, God filled the house with His cloud in order to remind the celebrants that, regardless of all the physical phenomena taking place, (the singers, the trumpets, etc.) they were not to forget that it is God who is important, not the celebrants, however fervent they might be, and not the celebration per se, no matter how cleverly it is orchestrated

2 Chronicles 7: 5 – "And king Solomon offered a sacrifice of twenty and two thousand oxen, and a hundred and twenty thousand sheep: so the king and all the people dedicated the house of God.

2 Chronicles 7: 6 – "And the priests waited on their offices: the Levites also with instruments of music of the Lord, which David the king had made to praise the Lord, because his mercy endureth for ever, when David praised by their ministry; and the priests sounded trumpets before them, and all Israel stood."

(sta) 57. - Figuratively, and for all practical purposes, literally, when the trumpets sounded at the dedication ceremony opening the temple at Jerusalem, an entire nation, Israel, God's chosen people, stood, and united in spirit, acknowledged and worshiped the one true God.

2 Chronicles, Chapter 13 speaks of the war between Abijah and Jeroboam wherein the obedient people of Judah led by Abijah oppose the disobedient people of Israel led by Jeroboam.

Although the forces of Israel (800,00) greatly outnumbered those of Judah (400.000), Abijah excoriated Israel for rebelling against the Lord, removing duly authorized priests appointed in accordance Davidic propriety and for attempting to preempt the divinely ordained order of kingly succession.

2 Chronicles 13: 10 – "But as for us, the Lord is our God, and we have not forsaken him; and the priests, which minister unto the Lord, are the sons of Aaron, and the Levites wait upon their business: *

* *- (The Levites serve the priests as required in order to perform their duties.)*

Abijah further chastises Jeroboam by extolling the virtuous behavior of Judah by citing the proper behavior of her priests and the Levites who assist them:

2 Chronicles 13; 11 – "And they burn unto the Lord every morning and every evening burnt sacrifices and sweet incense: the showbread also they set in order upon the pure table; and the candlestick of gold with the lamps thereof to burn every evening: for we keep the charge of our Lord our God; but ye have forsaken him."

2 Chronicles 13: 12 - "And, behold, God himself is with us for our captain, and his priests with sounding <u>trumpets</u> *to cry alarm against you. O children of Israel, fight ye not against the Lord God of your fathers; for ye shall not prosper."*

(sta) 58. - When the army of Israel demonstrated intention to attack Judah, Abijah caused the trumpets of Judah to sound, virtually as warning from God to cease and desist their futile attempts at dictating which persons and procedures were acceptable in the eyes of God to properly worship Him.

But Abijah's entreaties fell on deaf ears. Jeroboam persisted. His battle tactics were successful in setting a trap, causing the army of Judah to be pinned down, surrounded by the army of Israel.

2 Chronicles 13: 14 – "And when Judah looked back, behold, the battle was before and behind: and they cried unto the Lord, and the priests sounded with the <u>trumpets</u>."

(sta) 59. – The final trumpet of the war between Abijah and Jeroboam, between Judah and Israel, sounded the death knell of a nation gone wrong- Israel), and the ascendancy of a nation-(Judah) obedient to God's will.

What follows next as described in 2 Chronicles 13: 15-20 provides vivid, powerful testimony of God's inexorable will. His kingdom will come, and His Will, will be done. To believe otherwise is not wise; to act contrary to God's will is spiritually deadening, and sometimes physically lethal:

<u>*2 Chronicles 13: 15-20*</u>

13: 15 – "Then the men of Judah gave a shout: and as the men of Juda shouted, it came to pass, that God smote Jeroboam and all Israel before Abijah and Judah."

13: 16 – And the children of Israel fled before Judah: and God delivered them into their hand."

13: 17 – "And Abijah and his people slew them with a great slaughter: so there fell down slain of Israel five hundred thousand chosen men."

13: 18 – "Thus the children of Israel were brought under at that time, and the children of Judah prevailed, because they relied upon the Lord God of their fathers."

13: 19 – "And Abijah pursued after Jeroboam, and took cities from him, Beth-el with the towns thereof, and Jeshanah with the towns thereof, and Ephrain with the towns thereof."

13: 20 – "Neither did Jeroboam recover strength again in the days of Abijah: and the Lord struck him, and he died."

(sta) 60. - When the destruction of Judah by Israel seemed imminent and unstoppable, the trumpets sounded and God listened.

The next occurrence of God dealing directly with the enemies of Judah, wherein the trumpet sound plays a significant role, is described in 2 Chronicles, chapter 20. Judah's king Jehoshaphat receives some disturbing news:

2 Chronicles 20: 1 – "It came to pass after this also, that the children of Moab, and the children of Ammon, and with them other beside the Ammonites, came against Jehoshaphat to battle."

2 Chronicles 20: 2 – "Then there came some that told Jehoshaphat, saying,

There cometh a great multitude against thee from beyond the sea on this side Syria; and behold they be in Hazazon-tamar, which is Engedi."

In response to these warnings, king Jehoshaphat laid his case before the Lord by prayer and worship, pleading for deliverance from the invading horde of the children of Ammon and Moab and mount Seir. Previously God had not allowed Israel to invade these nations when Moses led them out of Israel. But now, these same people want to oust Israel from this land promised them by God.

In answer to Judah's cry for help, God the Spirit came into Jahaziel the son of Zechariah, and spoke thru him to all of Judah:

2 Chronicles 20: 15 – "… Be not afraid nor dismayed by reason of this great multitude; for the battle is not yours, but God's."

When Judah and the inhabitants of Jerusalem, and singers appointed by Jehoshaphat began to sing and praise the Lord, the Lord God sewed confusion amongst the ranks of the enemy so that the children of Ammon and Moab stood up against the inhabitants of mount Seir,

"utterly to destroy them: and when they had made an end of the inhabitants of mount Seir, every man helped to destroy another." – 2 Chronicles 20: 23

Every man of Judah led by Jehoshaphat returned to Jerusalem:

20: 28 – "And they came to Jerusalem with psalteries and harps and <u>trumpets</u> unto the house of the Lord."

(sta) 61. – Psalteries –(small harps, and larger harps, all utilized for their soothing sounds) and the trumpets, which, depending on how played could be soothing to the nerves, or shrill, and sometimes blared with ear shattering volume, were brought into the temple at Jerusalem to mark and celebrate Judah's great victory over Moab, Ammon and others.

Because of divine intervention, Jehoshaphat and the armies of Judah had not been required to lift a finger to accomplish this startling victory. It was nevertheless Judah's victory, a victory of faith and obedience to the one true God, over the forces of non-believers and idolaters.

Taking a page, thousands of years in advance from the genre of treachery, greed, murder and mayhem that is so aptly portrayed in the current, vastly popular series Game of Thrones, was a lady named Athaliah.

Upon learning that her son, the wicked king Ahaziah had been killed by a man named Jehu whom the Lord had appointed to cut off the house of Ahab, Athaliah arose and destroyed all the royal seed of the house of Judah, thereby eliminating any potential heirs to the royal throne of Judah.

But, and there always seems to be a but in these kingly competitions, the daughter of the slain king Ahaziah-(her name was Jeho-shabeath) managed to hide Joash the secret infant son of Ahaziah, the true heir to the throne of Judah and hide him away for six years. For all these six years the infamous Athaliah reigned over the land.

But when Joash reached the age of seven years, the priest Jehoiada engineered a coup, a fait accompli whereby Joash (seven years of age) was proclaimed king of Judah:

2 Chronicles 23: 13 – "And she looked and behold, the king stood at his pillar at the entering in, and the princes and the <u>trumpets</u> by the king: and all the people of the land rejoiced, and sounded with <u>trumpets</u>, also the singers with instruments *of music, and such as taught to sing praise. Then Athaliah rent her clothes, and said, Treason, treason."*

(sta) 62. - Jehoiada choreographed the final scene of Athaliah's downfall and Joash's ascension so that when Athaliah entered the temple to ascertain what all the fuss was about, there stood the newly minted king Joash, celebrated by singers and musical instruments, his kingship undeniably affirmed by the trumpets great blare.

And despite her heated protestations, the wicked queen Athaliah received her just rewards. As recorded in the final verse of 2 Chronicles, chapter 23, not only did she lose her queenhood, she lost her life:

2 Chronicles 23: 15 –"So they laid hands on her; and when she was come to the entering of the horse gate by the king's house, they slew her there."

(sta) 63. – At the second sounding of the trumpets Athaliah tore her clothes and cried treason. And that was her final earthly defiance of God's will. Instead of accepting the inevitable execution of 'His Will Be Done', she did not repent, she did not ask for God's forgiveness, nor did she proclaim or exhibit determination to sin no more.

2 Chronicles, chapter 29, verses 1-36 recalls the sanctification of Judah, inspired and led by king Hezekiah who reigned over Judah for 29 years. In the very first year of his reign at 25 yrs. of age, Hezekiah gathered together the priests and the Levites, commanding them to undo the wrongs of the fathers by sanctifying themselves and the temple. All filth, spiritual and physical must be cleansed. All sacrifices and rituals ordained by the Lord God of Israel must be restored. Hezekiah reminds them that as a result of those past transgressions:

2 Chronicles 29: 8-9 - "Wherefore the wrath of the Lord was upon Judah and Jerusalem, and he hath delivered them to trouble, to astonishment, and to hissing as ye see with you eyes.

For, lo, our fathers have fallen by the sword, and our sons and our daughters and our wives are in captivity for this."

The priests and the Levites complied fully with the king's commands:

The Levites reached out and assembled their brethren, and together with them, they sanctified themselves, and they came together to cleanse the temple.

The priests went from the outer to the inner parts of the temple, (even into the most inner part, the holy of holies) and removed all things offensive to God, – (particularly objects associated with idolatry) and the Levites brought these foul objects to Kidron * for disposal. They cleansed the outer and inner part of the house of the Lord; they cleansed and sanctified the sacred vessels that had been discarded by king Ahaz.

* - The valley of Kidron was used as a garbage dump wherein unclean objects were disposed of, usually by burning.

Then as atonement for Israel, king Hezekiah gathered together all the rulers of the city, and they went into the house of the Lord where a great celebration, a great feast, a great series of burnt offerings, and a grand worship were conducted:

2 Chronicle 29: 26 – "And the Levites stood with the instruments of David, and the priests stood with the <u>trumpets</u>."

2 Chronicles 29: 27 – "And Hezekiah commanded to offer the burnt offering upon the altar. And when the burnt offering began, the song of the Lord began also with the <u>trumpets</u>, and with the instruments ordained by David king of Israel."

2 Chronicles 29: 28 – And all the congregation worshiped, and the singers sang, and the <u>trumpeters</u> sounded: and all this continued until the burnt offering was finished,

(sta) 64. – The priest's helpers (the Levites) stood with the cymbals, psalteries, and with harps, and the priests stood with the trumpets at the occasion of the restoration of temple worship by king Hezekiah.

(sta) 65. - And when the burnt offerings began at the occasion of the restoration of temple worship by king Hezekiah, the song of the Lord began, and so too did the trumpets, along with the other instruments of invocation, gratitude and worship.

(sta) 66. – Whilst the tremendous numbers of burnt offerings were burning, the congregation worshiped and the trumpets sounded. At the occasion of the restoration of worship at the temple brought about by king Hezekiah, the singers had ample time to sing The Song of the Lord.

And so ends Chapter Fifteen

Chapter fifteen yields twelve significant trumpet associations:

(sta) 55. – Celebrating the installation of the Ark of God at Jerusalem, Israel experienced one of her finest moments:

She adhered to tradition, i.e., properly clad singers, duly authorized via custom and heritage, with their sons and brethren furnished with cymbals, psalteries, and harps, led by 120 priests playing the trumpets, united, one and all, worshiping the one true God, the God of Abraham, Isaac, and Jacob.

(sta) 56. – Celebrating the installation of the Ark of God at Jerusalem, the trumpeters and singers blended their sounds in a manner so as to create one voice, possibly constituting the first one-sound combination of trumpet/voice in praise and glory of God.

(sta) 57. - Figuratively, and for all practical purposes, literally, when the trumpets sounded at the dedication ceremony opening the temple at Jerusalem, an entire nation, Israel, God's chosen people, stood, and united in spirit, acknowledged and worshiped the one true God.

(sta) 58. - When the army of Israel demonstrated intention to attack Judah, Abijah caused the trumpets of Judah to sound, virtually as warning from God to cease and desist their futile attempts at dictating which persons and procedures were acceptable in the eyes of God to properly worship Him.

(sta) 59. – The final trumpet of the war between Abijah and Jeroboam, between Judah and Israel, sounded the death knell

of a nation gone wrong- (Israel), and the ascendancy of a nation-(Judah) obedient to God's will

(sta) 60. - When the destruction of Judah by Israel seemed imminent and unstoppable, the trumpets sounded and God listened.

(sta) 61. – Psalteries –(small harps, and larger harps, all utilized for their soothing sounds) and the trumpets, which, depending on how played, could be soothing to the nerves, or shrill, and sometimes blared with ear shattering volume, were brought into the temple at Jerusalem to mark and celebrate Judah's great victory over Moab, Ammon and others.

(sta) 62. - Jehoiada choreographed the final scene of Athaliah's downfall and Joash's ascension so that when Athaliah entered the temple to ascertain what all the fuss was about, there stood the newly minted king Joash, celebrated by singers and musical instruments, his kingship undeniably affirmed by the trumpets great blare.

(sta) 63. – At the second sounding of the trumpets Athaliah tore her clothes and cried treason. And that was her final earthly defiance of God's will. Instead of accepting the inevitable execution of 'His Will Be Done', she did not repent, she did not ask for God's forgiveness, nor did she proclaim or exhibit determination to sin no more.

(sta) 64. – The priest's helpers (the Levites) stood with the cymbals, psalteries, and with harps, and the priests stood with the trumpets at the occasion of the restoration of temple worship by king Hezekiah.

(sta) 65. - And when the burnt offerings began at the occasion of the restoration of temple worship by king Hezekiah, the song of the Lord began, and so too did the trumpets, along with the other instruments of invocation, gratitude and worship.

(sta) 66. – Whilst the tremendous numbers of burnt offerings were burning, the congregation worshiped and the trumpets sounded. At the occasion of the restoration of worship at the temple brought about by king Hezekiah, the singers had ample time to sing The Song of the Lord. *

Notes and Reflections

_____
_____
_____
_____
_____
_____
_____
_____
_____
_____
_____
_____
_____
_____
_____
_____
_____
_____
_____
_____
_____
_____
_____
_____
_____
_____
_____
_____
_____
_____
_____

Chapter Sixteen

Significant trumpet associations derived from the book of Ezra

Although not a believer, Cyrus the king of Persia was nevertheless motivated to allow the Jewish captives in his conquered territories to return to Jerusalem, and to build the temple there:

1 Ezra 1-3

"Now in the first year of Cyrus king of Persia, that the word of the Lord by the mouth of Jeremiah might be fulfilled, the Lord stirred up the spirit of Cyrus king of Persia, that he made a proclamation throughout all his kingdom, and put it also in writing, saying,

Thus saith Cyrus king of Persia, The Lord God of heaven hath given me all the kingdoms of the earth; and he hath charged me to build him a house in Jerusalem, which is in Judah.

Who is there among you of all his people? His God be with him, which let him go up to Jerusalem, which is in Judah, and build the house of the Lord God of Israel (he is the God,) which is in Jerusalem."

Ezra 3: 10 – "And when the builders laid the foundation of the temple of the Lord, they set the priests in their apparel with <u>trumpets</u>, and the Levites the sons of Asaph with cymbals, to praise the Lord, after the ordinance of David king of Israel."

As a result of king Cyrus' edicts, the rebuilding of the temple was begun, worship at the house of God resumed with the priests blowing the trumpets, while the Levites clanged the cymbals.

(sta) 67. - The trumpets blare served to pronounce the restoration of worship at the temple in Jerusalem.

And so ends Chapter Sixteen.

Chapter sixteen yields one significant trumpet association:

(sta) 67. – The trumpets blare served to pronounce the restoration of worship at the temple in Jerusalem.

Notes and Reflections

Chapter Seventeen

Significant trumpet associations derived from the book of Nehemiah

The Old Testament book of Nehemiah, (written by Nehemiah himself) tells the story of the rebuilding of the walls of Judah; said walls purposed to provide protection for the nation of Judah and for its capital, Jerusalem.

When Nehemiah learned of the decrepit condition of these allegedly protective walls, he was inspired to see to their repair. And this he eventually did accomplish, but not without overcoming fierce opposition from a man named Sanballat, the governor of Samaria.

Despite Sanballat's efforts, which included trickery and mockery, and numerous attempted murders of the Jewish workers by Sanballat's cohorts, the walls of Judah were fully repaired in 52 days.

Nehemiah 4: 18, 20

4: 18 – "For the builders, every one had his sword girded by his side, and so builded. And he that sounded the trumpet was by me."

4: 20 - "In what place therefore ye hear the sound of the <u>trumpet</u>, resort ye thither unto us: our God shall fight for us."

Every Jew engaged in the rebuilding of the walls of Judah was armed with a sword. Additionally, Nehemiah had a trumpeter at the ready to call for reinforcements if an attack should occur.

The plan Nehemiah set in place was this, that at the instant of the trumpets blare, the wall-workers-turned-soldiers would drop their spades, grasp their swords and hasten to the trumpet's call for help.

(sta) 68. - Not only was the trumpet sound a call for help, but during the rebuilding of the walls of Judah, it also served as a reminder to those working on the wall that God was on their side and would fight for them.

Finally, after all the difficulties, the trials and hardships endured by Nehemiah and the rebuilders of the walls of Judah, their work was done and the dedication ceremony proceeded.

12: 35 – "And certain of the priests' sons with <u>trumpets</u>; namely Zechariah the son of Jonathan, the son of Shemaiah, the son of Mattaniah, the son of Michaiah, the son of Zaccur, the son of Asaph:"

12: 41 - "And the priests; Eliakim, Maaseiah, Miniamin, Michaiah, Elioenai, Zechariah, and Haniah, with <u>trumpets</u>."

(sta) 69. – At the dedication ceremony celebrating the rebuilding of the walls of Judah, priests, and the sons of priests were tasked with the blowing of the trumpets.

And so ends Chapter Seventeen.

Chapter seventeen yields two significant trumpet associations:

(sta) 68. - Not only was the trumpet sound a call for help, but during the rebuilding of the walls of Judah, it also served as a reminder of Nehemiah's promise to those working on the wall that God would fight for them. The trumpet sound can serve as a reminder to the faithful that God is with them.

(sta) 69. – At the dedication ceremony celebrating the rebuilding of the walls of Judah, priests and the sons of priests were tasked with the blowing of the trumpets, thereby demonstrating that trumpets were often used in religious ceremonies and other important occasions.

Notes and Reflections

_____
_____
_____
_____
_____
_____
_____
_____
_____
_____
_____
_____
_____
_____
_____
_____
_____
_____
_____
_____
_____
_____
_____
_____
_____
_____
_____
_____
_____

Chapter Eighteen

Significant trumpet associations derived from the book of Job

The author of the Old Testament book of Job is unknown. Some scholars opine that Moses wrote it, but the book does not identify the author.

One of the main purposes of God's relationship with Job as recorded in the Bible is to demonstrate the inadequacy of humankind to reason out, or to somehow account for those occasions when the innocent of this world are allowed to suffer. One of the conclusions that should be drawn from this demonstration is that mankind must totally commit to an attitude of complete trust in, and dependence upon God whose workings man cannot fathom.

In the book of 'Job' God allows Satan to put Job to the test. Is Job truly what God claims him to be – righteous, humble, and grateful, or is he as Satan claims, avaricious, proud, and ungrateful of God's bounty?

Job 1: 8 – "And the Lord said unto Satan, Hast thou considered my servant Job, that there is none like him in the earth, a perfect and an upright man, one that feareth God, and escheweth evil?"

Or is Job simply happy and appreciative of all the worldly goods and family blessings that God has bestowed upon him? Satan challenges God thusly:

Job 1: 11 - "But put forth thy hand now, and touch all that he hath, and he will curse thee to thy face."

God responds to this challenge by allowing Satan to test Job, but not to the extent of subjecting him to physical abuse:

Job 1: 12 – "And the Lord said unto Satan, Behold, all that he hath is in thy power; only upon himself put not thy hand. So Satan went forth from the presence of the Lord."

There is an important lesson to be learned from God's caveat to Satan when allowing him to test Job, i.e., Satan is not allowed to physically harm Job.

It does not take s great leap of reasoning to conclude that physical torture and abuse, when used to force someone to renounce their faith does not constitute a valid renunciation of faith by the abused believer.

To those who fear they would be unable to withstand physical abuse, and/or mental torture in defense of their faith; rest assured that God loves you and would not forsake you for forsaking Him under circumstances of such extreme duress.

Some scholars believe that the book of Job, except for the first early chapters of Genesis is the oldest written book of the Bible, and that Moses wrote it. Perhaps the lessons to be learned from reading Job are of such importance that the Holy Spirit inspired Moses to set the record of Job's trial early on so as to have a greater impact.

Job is sorely tested: All his earthly wealth and family blessings are taken away, and/or destroyed. He is unaware of course of why all these bad things are happening or what he has done, or not done to deserve such treatment. God does not put an end to Job's suffering so easily, not until Job finally realizes the lessons of the testing, to wit:

Mankind has inadequate reasoning ability to account for the suffering of the innocent, and should embrace an attitude of complete trust and dependence on God whose workings cannot be fathomed.

Chapter 39 of Job tells us that in response to Job's continued incomprehension of what is going on, God continues to challenge him on all manner of subjects relating to Job's knowledge and power of them vis-à-vis God's knowledge and power. For example verses 19 through 25 continues a series of rhetorical questions directed to Job, this time regarding his knowledge of, and power over horses:

Job 39: 19-25

"Hast thou given the horse strength? Hast thou clothed his neck with thunder?

Canst thou make him afraid as a grasshopper? The glory of his nostrils is terrible.

He paweth in the valley, and rejoiceth in his strength: he goeth on to meet the armed men.

He mocketh at fear, and is not afrighteth; neither turneth he back from the sword.

The quiver rattleth against him, the glittering spear and the shield.

He swalloweth the ground with fierceness and rage: neither believeth he that it is the sound of the <u>trumpet</u>.

He saith among the <u>trumpets</u>, Ha ha ! And he smelleth the battle afar off, the thunder of the captains, and the shouting."

(sta) 70. – God extolls the virtues of one of his created creatures, the warhorse, pointing out that this fearsome animal disregards the danger signaled by the blaring trumpets.

(sta) 71. –As the trumpets blare comes closer and closer, and their fearsome scream grows louder and louder, the warhorse understands what they mean, but true to its created nature it paws the ground in destiny fulfilling anticipation.

These questions are a challenge to Job by God. Of course Job has no power over a horse or knowledge of how a horse came to be a horse. The accumulative realization by Job of his total inability to account for the whys and wherefores of God's creations, particularly of God's created creatures leaves him dumbfounded until the crushing weight of the inferential evidence that has been presented to him convinces Job of the utter futility of questioning the Creator's wisdom, purpose and love. As we read in chapter 42, Job finally and completely submits to God:

Job 42: 1-3

"I know that thou canst do anything, and that no thought can be withholden from thee.

Who is he who hideth counsel without knowledge? Therefore have I uttered that I understood not; things too wonderful for me, which I knew not."

Job 42: 5-6

"I have heard of thee by the hearing of the ear; but now mine eye seeth thee:

Wherefore I abhor myself, and repent in dust and ashes." *

* Heretofore Job understood and worshiped God with his physical mind and body. Now he sees God with his spirit's eye, more fully appreciating God's purpose, wisdom, and mysterious ways.

And so ends Chapter Eighteen

Chapter eighteen yields two significant trumpet associations:

(sta) 70. – God extolls the virtues of one of his created creatures, the warhorse, pointing out that this fearsome animal disregards the danger signaled by the blaring trumpets.

(sta) 71. –As the trumpets blare comes closer and closer, and their fearsome scream grows louder and louder, the warhorse knows what they portend, but true to its created nature it paws the ground in destiny fulfilling anticipation.

Notes and Reflections

Chapter Nineteen

Significant trumpet associations derived from the Book of Psalms.

The Book of Psalms constitutes a record of laments, thanksgivings, and praises of the Lord God of Israel by his chosen people Israel.

All told there are 150 Psalms. The longest one is Psalm No.119 having 176 verses, while Psalm No. 117 is the shortest with just two.

Wikipedia defines psalm, and Book of Psalms as follows:

Psalm - a sacred song or hymn, in particular any of those contained in the biblical Book of Psalms and used in Christian and Jewish worship;

Book of Psalms - a book of the Bible comprising a collection of religious verses, sung or recited in both Jewish and Christian worship. Many are traditionally ascribed to King David.

For the reason that trumpets play significant roles as recorded in four psalms, we will concern ourselves and deal briefly with Psalm Nos. 47, 81, 98, and 150.

Psalm 47: 5 – "God is gone up with a shout, the Lord with the sound of the __trumpet__."

There is much discussion regarding on which of the occasions when God has "gone up" that this verse refers to, but it appears to be prophetically speaking of when Jesus comes again and prepares to reign as King of Kings, and Lord of Lord over all the earth. Specifically, at the Rapture of his church Jesus will descend midst the clouds of heaven. Those who died in faith will rise up to meet him with new and perfect spiritual bodies, and then those living in faith at that time will also rise to meet him with new and perfect spiritual bodies. Together, Jesus and his raptured church will ascend to heaven. Jesus will rise for the second time. - (The first time was at the Resurrection.)

*(sta) 72. - Giving due consideration to Psalm 47: 5, to the accompanying commentary and to other sources * might reasonably lead to the conclusion that there (were-are-will be) occasions when the trumpet sound is closely associated with the comings and goings, or more specifically, to the descending and rising of God.*

* - Other sources –e.g., as in the Book of Genesis, chapter 17, verse 3, indicates that after God left off talking with Abraham, He went up to heaven, or, as recorded in *2 Samuel, chapter 6, verse 15:*

"So, David and all the house of Israel brought up the ark of the Lord with shouting, and with the sound of the trumpet."

Psalm 81 speaks of God's goodness, Israel's transgressions, and God's demand for Israel's obedience.

It reminds Israel of her past misdeeds, particularly of the frequent lapses into idol worship. God recalls how he delivered the people from their bondage, and how, due to their refusal to worship only the one true God, God was denied the pleasure of treating his chosen people in the royal manner he had planned. That old-devil 'free will' had frequently interfered.

Each autumn at the time of the new moon the trumpet sound ushered in a period of cultic rituals. Two weeks later, with the arrival of the full moon, the trumpets blare signaled the end of these activities.

Psalm 81: 3 – "Blow up the trumpet in the new moon, in the time appointed, on our solemn feast day."

(sta) 73. – In addition to their other functions, trumpets were used to signal the opening and closing of ritualistic religious ceremonies.

Psalm 98 is unabashedly happy and celebratory, praising God and expressing gratitude to the Lord for making Israel God's chosen people. Verse 6 records the role played by the trumpets:

Psalm 98: 6 – "With the trumpets and sound of cornet make a joyful noise before the Lord, the King."

Psalm 150, the final psalm, is a pure hymn of praise for the Lord. Verse 3 records the role played by the trumpets contributing to that praise:

Psalm 150: 3 – "Praise him with the sound of the trumpet: praise him with the psaltery and harp."

(sta) 74. - Particularly when used during sacred songs (psalms), the use of trumpets helped foster the attainment of a personal relationship with God commensurate with the emotional intensity associated with fervent prayer.

Psalm 150, verse 6 is the final verse of The Book of Psalms. It expresses beautifully the dominant theme of The Book of Psalms:

Psalm 150: 6 - "Let everything that hath breath praise the Lord. Praise ye the Lord."

And so ends Chapter Nineteen

Chapter Nineteen yields three significant trumpet associations:

(sta) 72. – From this and other sources it is becomes more apparent that the trumpet sound is closely associated with the comings and goings, or more specifically, to the descending and rising of Jesus the Christ, the Son of God.

(sta) 73. – In addition to their other functions, trumpets were used to signal the opening and closing of ritualistic religious ceremonies.

(sta) 74. - Particularly when used during sacred songs (psalms), the use of trumpets helped foster the attainment of a personal relationship with God commensurate with the emotional intensity associated with fervent prayer.

Notes and Reflections

_____
_____
_____
_____
_____
_____
_____
_____
_____
_____
_____
_____
_____
_____
_____
_____
_____
_____
_____
_____
_____
_____
_____
_____
_____

Chapter Twenty

Significant trumpet associations derived from the Book of Isaiah

Isaiah 18: 3 – "All ye inhabitants of the world, and dwellers on the earth, see ye, when he lifteth up an ensign on the mountains; and when he bloweth a <u>trumpet</u>, hear ye."

* - Verse 3 of Isaiah 18 can be considered as referring directly to the main theme of the chapter wherein it is recorded that Isaiah correctly prophesizes the defeat of Ethiopia by Assyria 200 years in advance of the actual happening.

Indirectly, but no less valid than the specific connection to the defeat of Ethiopia, Isaiah, chapter 18, verse 3 reminds us not to ignore the fact that God is instrumental in all of earth's history.

The history of war, starting with the early years of planet earth, (as recorded in Genesis, chapter 14) right up until the time of Isaiah, and continuing to the present age reveals certain truths regarding war. For example, when an aggressor army proudly displays the ensign associated with its national identity such as a hammer and sickle, and trumpets (loudly broadcasts) its bogus justifications for engaging in warfare, you can be sure that by that stage of negotiations, diplomacy has devolved into long-winded futility.

Once the enemy can no longer hide its true colors or otherwise decides that it is disadvantageous to do so, it will flaunt the ensign of its armies, declare (trumpet) its alleged justifications, and proceed to conduct war.

An ensign is frequently a symbol used to whip up patriotic fervor to a degree wherein commonsense and the sense of right and wrong are greatly diminished or completely ignored.

(sta) 75. – When an army's ensign is displayed and its trumpets blare, or otherwise aggressively bellow justification for warfare, sooner or later, war is coming; sooner more likely than later.

Isaiah, chapter 27 speaks of when Jesus comes again and of the Kingdom age, the age that will follow this, the age of grace – (the age of the church). Jesus will cast Satan into hell's-fire and will rule the new heaven on earth. He will gather Israel under His wing in Jerusalem.

Isaiah 27: 13 – "And it shall come to pass in that day, that the great trumpet shall be blown, and they shall come which were ready to perish in the land of Assyria, and the outcasts in the land of Egypt, and shall worship the Lord in the holy mount at Jerusalem."

(sta) 76. – The great trumpet, probably a "shophar" - a trumpet fashioned from a ram's horn, will signal the beginning of God's actions, culminating in Israel's repenting of her past

rejections of Jesus and in the fulfillment of the Old and New Testament's promises of salvation for God's chosen people."

In addition to Isaiah 27: 13 ^, there are two other verses of Scripture (both of them in the N.T.) that foretell the blowing of trumpets when Jesus comes again to establish His kingdom on earth, *1 Thessalonians 4: 16 and Rev.11: 15:*

1 Thessalonians 4: 16 – "For the Lord himself shall descend from heaven with a shout, with the voice of the archangel, and with the trump of God: and the dead in Christ shall rise first."

*Revelation 11: 15 – "And the seventh angel sounded; and there were great voices in heaven saying, The kingdoms of the world are become the kingdoms of our Lord, and of his Christ; and he shall rein for ever and ever." **

* - Revelation 8: 2 (not shown here) informs us that the seventh angel sounded a trumpet.

These two verses will be considered and commented on as we encounter them in due course in Revelation, the final book of the New Testament and of the Bible.

In the final chapters of the book of Isaiah, Isaiah transitions from the previous chapters dealing with: condemnations of Israel, the calling of Isaiah, the future of the Nations, the tragedies and triumphs of the kingdom age, (including the great tribulation) the various woes to be suffered by those who will rebel against God, and recalling the history of Israel, to: the better times to come, the coming of the prince of peace, the character of the peace, and finally, to the consummation of peace.

But verse 1 of Chapter 58 continues the storm before the calm. God commands Isaiah to cry out to the people in a loud voice, a voice like the blast of a trumpet, and reminding them of their oft' repeated rebellious sins, such as idolatry, hypocrisy and pride:

Isaiah 58: 1 – "Isaiah 58: 1 – "Cry aloud, spare not, lift up thy voice like a <u>trumpet</u>, and shew my people their transgression, and the house of Jacob their sins."

(sta) 77. – To assure that Isaiah's words gain Israel's attention, God commands him to shout like the blast of a trumpet. In terms of getting attention and emphasizing the importance of what follows it, the trumpet sound had no equal in the Old Testament.

And so ends Chapter Twenty

Chapter twenty yields three significant trumpet associations:

(sta) 75. – When an army's ensign is displayed and its trumpets blare, or otherwise aggressively bellows justification for warfare, sooner or later war is coming; sooner more likely than later.

(sta) 76. – The great trumpet, probably a "shophar" - a trumpet fashioned from a ram's horn, will signal the beginning of God's actions, culminating in Israel's repenting of her past rejections of Jesus and in the fulfillment of the Old and New Testament's promises of salvation for God's chosen people."

(sta) 77. – to assure that Isaiah's words gain Israel's attention, God commanded him to shout like the blast of a trumpet. In terms of getting attention and emphasizing the importance of what follows it, the trumpet sound had no equal in the Old Testament.

Notes and Reflections

_____
_____
_____
_____
_____
_____
_____
_____
_____
_____
_____
_____
_____
_____
_____
_____
_____
_____
_____
_____
_____
_____
_____
_____
_____
_____
_____
_____
_____
_____

Chapter Twenty-One

Significant trumpet associations derived from the book of Jeremiah

Chapter 4 of the book of Jeremiah continues God's actions designed to persuade Judah to forego her ways of apostasy and idolatry: In verses 1 & 2, recorded below, God promises Judah that as a reward for proper behavior, (in particular the discontinuance of idolatry) Judah will not be removed from God's presence. In addition, God's promise to Abraham, (as recorded in the book of Genesis) that all the Nations (non-Jews) would also be blessed because of Abraham, would be realized:

Jeremiah 4: 1, 2

4: 1 – If thou wilt return, O Israel, saith the Lord, return unto me: and if thou wilt put away thine abominations out of my sight, then shalt not thou remove.

4: 2 – "And thou shalt swear, The Lord liveth, in truth, in judgment, and in righteousness; and the nations shall bless themselves in him, and in him shall they glorify."

Jeremiah 4: 4 – "Circumcise yourselves to the Lord, and take away the foreskins of your heart, ye men of Judah and inhabitants of Jerusalem: lest my fury come forth like fire, and burn that none can quench it, because of the evil of your doings.

Verse 4: 4 constitutes a severe admonition from the Lord to Judah: prepare yourselves; cut away the layers hard-heartedness, the result of repeated disobedience of God's laws and of multiple occasions of idol worship and apostasy; get on board with the Lord, dangerous times are coming:

Jeremiah 4: 5 – "Declare ye in Judah, and publish in Jerusalem; and say, Blow ye the <u>trumpet</u> in the land: cry, gather together, and say, Assemble yourselves, and let us go into the defensed cities."

(sta) 78. - At a time of danger of attack from the North, (the Babylonians) Isaiah calls for the blowing of the trumpets to serve as a call for national self-examination, and as an urgent call to assemble concurrent with the necessity of withdrawing to fortified cities:

Because of Judah's wickedness, destruction approaches. The Lord reminds Judah that her punishment is a just punishment; that they are the cause of their own punishment. Judah's cognizance of her justifiable guilt in the eyes of the Lord pierces her very soul. Jeremiah laments:

Jeremiah 4: 19 - "My bowels, my bowels! I am pained at my very heart; my heart maketh a noise in me; I cannot hold my peace, because thou hast heard O my soul, the sound of the <u>trumpet</u>, the alarm of war."

(sta) 79. - Sometimes the trumpet sound is thought to be synonymous with the alarm of war, or even, given its unmistakable association with battles, with the sound and fury of pitched battles, the clash of weapons, the frightening sounds of wounded men crying, and the last gasps of soldiers dying.

Jeremiah 4: 20-21

"Destruction upon destruction is cried; for the whole land is spoiled: suddenly are my tents spoiled, and my curtains in a moment."

How long shall I see the standard, and hear the sound of the trumpet?"

(sta) 80 - Wars and rumors of wars can arrive in the blink of an eye, but once the war arrives, the enemy insignia can remain on display and the war trumpets can blare, for what seem like a lifetime. For those who die, it is a lifetime.

Jeremiah 4: 22 – "For my people is foolish, they have not known me; they are sottish children, and they have none understanding: they are wise to do evil, but to do good they have no knowledge." *

* - Although Jeremiah loves Judah and her people, he considers them to be as willful, disobedient children, i.e., "sottish". This word is found only in the KJV of the bible and only in this one instance.

Jeremiah 6: 1 – "O ye children of Benjamin, gather yourselves to flee out of the midst of Jerusalem, and blow the trumpet in Tekoa, and set up a sign of fire in Bethhaccerem: for evil appeareth out of the north, and great destruction." *

* - Tekoa in Judah was a fortification whose task it was, to be on guard against invasion and to sound warning alarms.

Bethhaccerem, a village nearby to Jerusalem was equipped and tasked to ignite fires in order to warn of approaching hostiles.

(sta) 81. - The threat to Judah of invasions was a constant, and so too was the necessity of having trumpets and bonfires available at a moment's notice for the purposes of warning, mobilization and preparation for war.

Jeremiah 6: 17 – "Also I set watchmen over you, saying, Hearken to the sound of the <u>trumpet</u>. But they said, We will not hearken."*

* - The watchmen were prophets assigned the specific task of sounding warning trumpets.

(sta) 82. - Provisions were well established to afford adequately early warnings to Judah of impending battles via trumpets, but incredibly the people declined to cooperate. They would not hearken; they would not obey the commands of the Lord.

The incredible, stiff-necked arrogance and stubbornness of God's chosen people is almost beyond belief. Their repeated obstinacy stirred our Lord to righteous anger as exemplified by the following five verses:

<u>Jeremiah 6: 18-22</u>

"Therefore hear, ye nations, and know O congregation, what is among them.

Hear, O earth; behold I will bring evil upon this people, even the fruit of their thoughts, because they have not hearkened unto my word, nor to my law, but rejected it.

To what purpose cometh there to me incense from Sheba, and the sweet cane from a far country? Your burnt offerings are not acceptable, nor your sacrifices sweet unto me.

Therefore thus saith the Lord, Behold, I will lay stumbling blocks before this people, and the fathers and the sons together shall fall upon them, the neighbor and his friends shall perish.

Thus saith the Lord, behold a people cometh from the north country, and a great nation shall be raised from the sides of the earth.

They shall lay hold on bow and spear; they are cruel, and have no mercy; their voice roareth like the sea; and they ride upon horses, set in array as men for war against thee, O daughter of Zion."

And then again a little further along in the book of Jeremiah, we learn of yet another instance of bold refusal to trust in the word of the Lord. Instead of obeying God by remaining in the land, which He had given them, the leaders and people of Judah choose to do otherwise. They decide to travel to Egypt, where they hoped to find refuge from the armies of the king of Babylon. The following few verses from the book of Jeremiah provide a brief sketch of these intransigencies:

Jeremiah transmits God's plans to Judah:

Jeremiah 42: 11 - "Be not afraid of the king of Babylon, of whom ye are afraid; be not afraid of him, saith the Lord: for I am with you to save you, and to deliver you from his hand."

Jeremiah 42: 12 – "And I shall show mercies unto you, that he may have mercy upon you, and cause you to return to your land."

Jeremiah 42: 13 – "But if ye say, we will not dwell in this land, neither obey the voice of the Lord your God,"

Jeremiah 42: 14 – "Saying, No; but we will go into the land of Egypt, where we shall see no war, nor hear the sound of the <u>trumpet</u>, nor have hunger of bread; and there will we dwell:"

Jeremiah 42: 16 – "Then it shall come to pass that the sword, which ye feared shall overtake you there in the land of Egypt, and the famine, whereof ye were afraid, shall follow close after you there in Egypt; and there ye shall die."

Nevertheless, and despite these dire warnings, the book of Jeremiah, chapter 43 tells us of some very bad decisions made by Johanan, and all the captains of the forces, and all the people of Judah: They decide to disobey the Lord:

Jeremiah 43: - So they came into the land of Egypt: for they obeyed not the voice of the Lord..." *

* - When skimming over the history of the Jews as related to its relationship with the Creator God, the question must come to mind: Why were the Jews so stubborn, stiff necked, proud, and disobedient to the will of God?

But when this question is asked, one must also ask: What group of people do we know of, who might have behaved better? In a manner of thinking, the second question answers the first.

(sta) 83. - The sounds of the trumpets of war had become synonymous with - (virtually, as terrible and fear inducing as the actuality of it) - the sounds and sights of war: the dead and the dying, the suffering of the wounded; their cries of pain and hopelessness, the silent despair, knowing that to survive intact meant to fight another day, or even synonymous with the hope of receiving a serious wound, but not too serious.

Jeremiah 44: 26-27 tells us of God's response to Judah's disobedience:

"Therefore hear ye the word of the Lord, all Judah that dwell in the land of Egypt; Behold, I have sworn by my great name, saith the Lord, that my name shall no more be named in the mouth of any man of Judah in all the land of Egypt, sayng, The lord God liveth.

Behold, I will watch over them for evil, and not for good: and all the men of Judah that are in the land of Egypt shall be consumed by the sword and by the famine, until there be an end to them."

However, the Lord allowed a small remnant of Jews to escape His wrath in Egypt and to return to Judah. In order to further impress on this remnant the certainty of God's will, the Lord will subject Egypt's pharaoh (under whose aegis the disobedient Jews had dwelled) into the hands of those who would kill him.

Chapter 51 of the book of Jeremiah describes the Lord's judgment against Babylon.

Verse 27 indicates the righteous anger of the Lord against Babylon and specifies certain instructions preparatory to the execution of His judgment:

Jeremiah 51: 27 – "Set up ye a standard in the land, blow the <u>trumpet</u> among the nations, prepare the nations against her, call together against her the kingdom of Ararat, Minni, and Ashchenaz; appoint a captain against her, cause the horses to come up as the rough caterpillars." *

* - A "standard," aka as an "ensign", is much like a flag, attached to a pole and raised so as to be visible from a distance, it is meant to inspire a tribe, a group of warriors or a nation to greater valor.

(sta) 84. - The spectacle of a standard flapping in the wind accompanied by the blare of a war trumpet had the potential of inspiring soldiers to perform deeds of great valor in battle. Such potential was sometimes realized, but not always.

And so ends Chapter Twenty-one

Chapter twenty-one yields seven significant trumpet associations:

(sta) 78. - At a time of danger of attack from the North, (the Babylonians) Isaiah calls for the blowing of the trumpets to serve as a call for national self-examination, and as an urgent call to assemble concurrent with the necessity of withdrawing to fortified cities:

(sta) 79. - Sometimes the trumpet sound is thought to be synonymous with the alarm of war, or even, given its unmistakable association with battles, with the sound and fury of pitched battles, the clash of weapons, the frightening sounds of wounded men crying, and the last gasps of soldiers dying.

(sta) 80 - Wars and rumors of wars can arrive in the blink of an eye, but once the war arrives, the enemy insignia can remain on display and the war trumpets can blare, for what seem like a lifetime. For those who die, it is a lifetime.

(sta) 81. - The threat to Judah of invasions was a constant, and so too was the necessity of having trumpets and bonfires available at a moment's notice for the purposes of warning, mobilization and preparation for war.

(sta) 82. - Provisions were well established to afford adequately early warnings to Judah of impending battles via trumpets, but incredibly the people declined to cooperate. They would not hearken; they would not obey the commands of the Lord

(sta) 83. - The sounds of the trumpets of war had become synonymous with - (virtually, as terrible and fear inducing as the actuality of it) - the sounds and sights of war: the dead and the dying, the suffering of the wounded; their cries of pain and hopelessness, the silent despair, knowing that to survive intact meant to fight another day, or even synonymous with the hope receiving a serious wound, but not too serious.

(sta) 84. - The spectacle of a standard flapping in the wind accompanied by the blare of a war trumpet had the potential of inspiring soldiers to perform deeds of great valor in battle. Such potential was sometimes realized, but not always.

Notes and Reflections

_____
_____
_____
_____
_____
_____
_____
_____
_____
_____
_____
_____
_____
_____
_____
_____
_____
_____
_____
_____
_____
_____
_____
_____
_____
_____
_____
_____
_____

Chapter Twenty-Two

Significant trumpet associations derived from the book of Ezekiel:

The author of the book of Ezekiel is Ezekiel the priest, the son of Buzi. Ezekiel began to prophesy when he was thirty years of age. Thirty years of age is the age at which a new priest was permitted to serve in that capacity.

Three years prior to that, as a captive of Nebuchadnezzar, he was deported to Babylon where he aspired to the priesthood, a status he attained at thirty years of age.

It is noteworthy that our Lord and Savior Jesus of Nazareth commenced His earthly ministry at twenty-seven years of age – (the same age as Ezekiel began training for the priesthood), and that at thirty years of age, - (the same age at which Ezekiel attained his goal of becoming a priest), Jesus attained His goal of dying on the cross as the ultimate blood-sacrifice – (the Lamb of God who taketh away the sins of the world). Although the Bible, all 66 Books of it, comprise thousands of years of spiritual history and was written by forty authors over a period of fifteen hundred years, the ages, dates and time-frames – (all expressed in numbers) are remarkably consistent, intertwined, and relative to each other, and are consistently expressive of biblical truths and foundational themes.

Once again, God's people had fallen into idol worship, disobedience, and disrespect of God Almighty. And now, in order to forestall impending annihilation, Israel causes the trumpets of war to blare. But God pronounces a terrible judgment against her: Don't bother with the customary preparations for upcoming battle; not trumpets, nor ensigns, nor hymns, nor blood sacrifices will save you:

Ezekiel 7: 14 -_– "They have blown the <u>trumpet</u>, even to make all ready; but none goeth to the battle: for my wrath is upon all the multitude thereof."

(sta) 85. – Trumpets may sound, but they carry out their intended effects only if it is God's will that they do so.

Once again the word of God comes to Ezekiel:

<u>*Ezekiel 33: 2-6*</u>

33: 2 - "Son of man, speak to the children of thy people, and say unto them, When I bring a sword upon a land, if the people of the land take a man of their coasts, and set him for their watchman:"

The people are instructed, that when they are threatened with attack righteously authorized by the Lord, they should assign one of their own as a watchman.

The Lord lays down the law regarding the people's responses to the trumpets sound, as spelled out in different scenarios:

Ezekiel 33: 3-4 - *"If when he seeth the sword come upon the land, he blow the trumpet, and warn the people;"*

Then whomsoever heareth the sound of the trumpet, and taketh not warning; if the sword come and take him away, his blood shall be upon his own head."

(sta) 86. - If, as has happened many times, the people of Israel choose to ignore God's commands (in this case His warning trumpet) and a weapon of war (either a physical sword or a spiritual lapse) injures physical, or spiritual lives, then it will be their own fault. Figuratively and literally, their own blood will be on their own hands.

Now, at this time of opportunity, if Israel heeds the word of God as relayed to them by Ezekiel, obeys God's commands and worships him only, they can evade the physical, and/or spiritual sword of God:

Ezekiel 33: 5 – "He heard the sound of the trumpet, and took not warning; his blood shall be upon him. But he that taketh warning shall deliver his soul."

(sta) 87 - He who heeds God's word, God's warning, God's trumpet; he will be saved physically and spiritually.

Ezekiel 33: 6 – "But if the watchman see the sword come, and blow not the trumpet, and the people be not warned; if the sword come, and take any person from among them, he is taken away in his iniquity; but his blood will I require at the watchman's hand.

(sta) 88. – If the watchman, cognizant of the imminent threat, fails in his duty to blow the trumpet, the people will

be judged regardless, and the watchman held accountable to carry out God's punishment against those so judged.

Every generation is burdened with false prophets. God will hold them accountable for not telling the people the truth, for not properly teaching the people of God's majesty and of his righteous anger at sinful behavior

Ezekiel always held true to God's words and informed Israel accordingly.

And so ends Chapter Twenty-two

Chapter twenty-two yields four significant trumpet associations:

(sta) 85. – Trumpets may sound, but they carry out their intended effects only if it is God's will that they do so.

(sta) 86. - If, as has happened many times, the people of Israel choose to ignore God's commands (in this case His warning trumpet) and a weapon of war (either a physical sword or a spiritual lapse) injures physical or spiritual lives, then it will be their own fault. Figuratively and literally, their own blood will be on their own hands.

(sta) 87 - He who heeds the word of God, the warning of God, the trumpet of God; he will be saved physically and spiritually.

(sta) 88. – If the watchman, cognizant of the imminent threat, fails in his duty to blow the trumpet, the people will be judged and the watchman held accountable for their physical and spiritual sentences.

Notes and Reflections

Chapter Twenty-Three

Significant trumpet associations derived from the book of Hosea:

Hosea 5: 8 - "Blow ye the cornet in Gibeah, and the trumpet in Ramah: cry aloud at Beth-aven, after thee, O Benjamin."

Once again Israel engages in idol worship and other sins of disobedience to the one, true God, and once more, via a prophet (Hosea) God causes warning trumpets to blare throughout Israel sounding the alarm: Cease and desist, stop your idol worship, obey my commands. I, your Lord, your God am a jealous God; I shall have no strange Gods before me.

(sta) 89. - Alas, Israel, as stiff-necked and stubborn as ever, refuses to even hear the word of God delivered by the trumpet's blare, never-mind, to actually heed it.

Now the predictable has begun: Israel forsakes the God of her creation; chooses instead to worship false Gods, and pledges allegiances to leaders far removed from spiritual values. The kingly line of David is abrogated. This generation of Israel will be punished by captivity and loss of freedom to worship. Israel is God's chosen people, and someday they will receive the opportunity of choosing

Jesus the Christ. At that time the remnant of them will choose correctly, but for now they will suffer captivity and separation from God.

8: 1 – "Set the <u>trumpet</u> to thy mouth. He shall come as an eagle against the house of the Lord, because they have transgressed against my law."

(sta) 90. - The time is now. The Assyrian enemy (depicted as an eagle) hovers over the house of Israel. Now! Blow the trumpet. Now!

And so ends Chapter Twenty-three

Chapter twenty-three yields 2 significant trumpet associations:

(sta) 89. - Alas, Israel, as stiff-necked and stubborn as ever, refuses to even hear the word of God delivered by the trumpet's blare, never-mind, to actually heed it.

(sta) 90. - The time is now. The Assyrian enemy (depicted as an eagle) hovers over the house of Israel. Now! Blow the trumpet. Now!

Although chapter Twenty- three proper ends with (sta's) 89 & 90 ^, two more segments of commentary relative to the text and sense of the chapter are included below: First, commentary on the Beatitudes, followed by commentary regarding Adam and Eve.

If we compare the situations that exist now in the United States and in the rest of the world with the conditions that existed in Israel at the time of the prophet Hosea, what similarities do we find?

The conditions of the world today, and the nation of Israel during the time of the prophet Hosea are strikingly similar. There exists now as then:

Lack of truth and honest relationships, nations-wide and individually.

Lack of mercy generally, and a total absence of mercy by an increasing number of groups and individuals are on the rise.

Eyes blind to the truth, and ears deaf to the word of God.

Rampant disconnect of people with God. Now, as then, this condition can be improved by daily reading of the Good Book.

National and personal decisions to pursue worldly values seem to be increasing exponentially.

National and personal decisions to pursue spiritual values seem to decrease at an alarming rate.

God frowns on deliberate drunkenness, and yet it is a state much sought after.

Noah, one of the greats of biblical history made the mistake of drinking too much:

Genesis 9: 21 – "And he drank of the wine, and was drunken: and he was uncovered within his tent."

* - The result of Noah's fall was that Ham, the father of Canaan saw his father Noah uncovered and told his brothers. They (Shem and Japheth) covered their father's nakedness. But it was not Ham who received a curse; rather it was Canaan, his son whom God relegated to a destiny of servitude to his brothers.

There have always been false prophets preaching false gospels: they claim to speak with the dead; they condone all kinds of conditions and actions shown to be displeasing to God; but worst of all they distract away from God. They (the false prophets) lie for profits. They encourage people to look for answers in all the wrong places. Directly and indirectly, false prophets try to influence you to reject Jesus Christ. How evil is that? They want you to reject "the way, the truth, and the life", the only path to salvation and eternal happiness.

Hosea was a prophet, chosen by God to preach a warning to the people of Israel, to alert them to the coming reign of punishment they were about to suffer at the hands of a hated enemy. The conditions that existed then exist now, particularly in this country. The question is: What must we do to be saved from God's righteous anger? The answer is, we must repent of our sins, believe in the Lord Jesus Christ, pray fervently for His divine mercy, and attempt to behave like true Christians.

If you are concerned about what it means to be a true Christian; how a true Christian should behave, clarity resides in the Holy Bible. Jesus tells us how we are to behave, and what the ideal attitudes of Christian life are. These ideals are called the Beatitudes.

Jesus travelled to a mount and taught the Beatitudes to the disciples, to the audience gathered there, and to all believers for all time. They are recorded in the New Testament book, the Gospel according to Matthew, chapter 5: verses 1-12.

In appreciation of the importance of the Beatitudes in Christian life, they are listed below as contained in an excerpt from my book, "Heaven On Earth", with accompanying commentary:

The Beatitudes

(The next eight codes (seven through fourteen) originate with Jesus as He begins what we now refer to as "The Sermon on the Mount." They are called "The Beatitudes", from the Latin word for blessed, "beatus."

Jesus promises a reward to those who spiritually personify each of the conditions identified by Him as "blessed." The Beatitudes exemplify how God wants us to behave, and are therefore, commandments of God.)

Matthew 5: 3 – Blessed are the poor in spirit: for theirs is the Kingdom of Heaven.

(In his epistle to other Jewish believers, James makes mention of "the poor", helping to clarify the spiritual status of those mentioned ^ as being "poor in spirit."

James 2: 5 – "Hearken, my beloved brethren, Hath not God chosen the poor of this world rich in faith, and heirs of the kingdom which he hath promised to them that love him?"

To be poor in spirit is to recognize our complete dependence on God.

To be poor in spirit is the antithesis of being proud, arrogant, and self-righteous.

In the gospel according to Luke, chapter 18, verses 10-14, Jesus tells the following parable to certain persons who were self-righteous, and arrogant:

"Two men went up into the temple to pray; the one a Pharisee, and the other a publican. The Pharisee stood and prayed thus with himself, God, I thank thee, that I am not as other men are, extortioners, unjust, adulterers, or even as this publican. *

I fast twice in the week, I give tithes of all that I possess.

And the publican, standing afar off, would not lift up so much as his eyes unto heaven, but smote upon his breast, saying, God be merciful to me a sinner.

I tell you, this man went down to his house justified rather than the other: for every one that exalteth himself shall be abased; and he that humbleth himself shall be exalted."

* - The Publicans were, more often than not, wealthy Romans who contracted with the government to collect taxes. However, this verse refers to those Jews employed by the Publicans to do the actual collecting of the various taxes imposed by Rome. Most Jews considered the collectors to be abettors of their oppressors, and despised them.

With deep humility and love of God, we must recognize that, absent God's divine grace, we are hopelessly lost. Those who acknowledge this fact and live accordingly are promised to participate in the Kingdom of Heaven.

The Beatitudes, and the other codes share a common foundation with all of Jesus' teachings in that they are based on spiritual reality. * Therefore they are in opposition to worldly ideals. They conflict with what would be our natural response patterns to adversity and challenges, but they are required of true Christians intent on obeying the commandments of God.

It takes extraordinary moral strength, and trust in God's will to be poor in spirit, and to attain all the states of blessedness expressed in the Beatitudes, but the reward is great. God, the Holy Spirit abiding in us makes it possible for us to obey the Beatitudes, and all the codes required to attain heaven on earth now, and in the world to come.

* - Evidence of the claim that spiritual reality is the basis for Jesus' teachings can be found in the gospel according to John:

The Chief rabbi, and the other temple leaders had complained to Pontius Pilate that Jesus claimed to be a king. If this proved to be true, Jesus would be guilty of treason against the Roman Empire, a crime punishable by death. During His three years ministry, Jesus had preached the gospel of repentance leading to salvation and citizenship in God's coming kingdom. As a result of the accusations of the Jews, Jesus is led to the hall of judgment where Pontius Pilate questions him:

John – 18: 33-38

"… Art thou the King of the Jews?

Jesus answers him,

"Sayest thou this thing of thyself, or did others tell it thee of me?

"Pilate answered, Am I a Jew? Thine own nation and the chief priests have delivered thee unto me: what hast thou done?

Jesus answered,

My kingdom is not of this world: if my kingdom were of this world, then would my servants fight, that I should not be delivered to the Jews: but now is my kingdom not from hence.

"Pilate therefore said unto him, Art thou a king then? Jesus answered,"

Thou sayest that I am a king. To this end was I born, and for this cause came I into the world, that I should bear witness unto the truth. Every one that is of the truth heareth my voice."

Matthew 5: 4 – Blessed are they that mourn: for they shall be comforted.

There are those who mourn because of terrible personal losses. There are those who mourn the state of the world, i.e. the wars, the sins, the injustices, the lack of civility, the selfishness etc.

To mourn over a personal loss is to demonstrate our love for the gifts God has given us, and have now passed on or changed.

To mourn over the condition of the world demonstrates our love for the way things should be, specifically, people behaving in accordance with the will of God.

The Book of Revelation contains a wonderful follow-up verse to Matthew 5: 4:

Revelation 7: 17 - "For the lamb which is in the midst of the throne shall feed them, and shall lead them unto living fountains of waters: and God shall wipe away all tears from their eyes."

We are to demonstrate our love of God by mourning the sinful condition of the world, and by lamenting the loss of those persons and situations He has given us to love.

To mourn is to experience deep sadness, and regret over the loss of a beloved person, place or thing. It is God's will that we do so, and it is His will that we bemoan the loss of the way this world would be if His will predominated.

Matthew 5: 5 –"Blessed are the meek: for they shall inherit the earth."

Those who are meek are not weak. They are strong in faith, and trust in God's will. They are humble before God, and gentle before people. There reward is great. They are heirs to God's estate, the new world to come, free of sin and strife.

It takes extraordinary moral strength, and trust in God's will, to be meek, and to attain all the states of blessedness expressed in the Beatitudes, but the reward is great. God, The Holy Spirit abiding in us makes it possible for us to obey the Beatitudes and all the codes required to attain heaven on earth now, and in the world to come.

Matthew 5: 6 – Blessed are they which do hunger and thirst after righteousness: for they shall be filled.

God wants us to spiritually yearn for good to prevail over evil, for ourselves and for the entire world. In order to demonstrate the intensity of this yearning, Jesus compares it to the physical conditions of being hungry and thirsty. Hunger for food, and thirst for water can be mild or strong, and so too can the desire for righteousness.

Jesus demonstrates just how strong the desire for righteousness can be, as found in the gospel according to Matthew, chapter 4, verses 1-4:

Matthew 4: 1-4

"Then was Jesus led up of the spirit into the wilderness to be tempted of the devil.

And when he had fasted forty days and forty nights, he was afterward an hungered.

And when the tempter came to him, he said, If thou be the Son of God, command that these stones be made bread. But he answered and said,

It is written, Man shall not live by bread alone, but by every word that proceedeth out of the mouth of God." *

* - After fasting for forty days and forty nights, Jesus was hungry. This statement is one of the great understatements of all time, and It helps emphasize Jesus' response to the devil, wherein He stresses the overriding importance of nourishing our spiritual lives with the word of God.

The phrase "an hungered" is an example of old English spelling and usage as featured in the King James Version of the bible.

It takes extraordinary moral strength, and trust in God's will to hunger and thirst after righteousness, and to attain all the states of blessedness expressed in the Beatitudes, but the reward is great. God, The Holy Spirit abiding in us makes it possible to obey the Beatitudes, and all the codes required to attain heaven on earth now, and in the world to come.

Matthew 5: 7 - Blessed are the merciful: for they shall obtain mercy.

If we show compassion to those who have offended us, (whether or not the offense was intentional) Jesus will have mercy on us. To be merciful is to admit that we are not perfect. Because of our sins and mistakes, we have hurt others. We, and they crave merciful forgiveness from God and man.

Along with a healthy dose of enlightened self-interest, it takes extraordinary moral strength, and trust in God's will to be merciful. The Holy Spirit abiding in us makes it possible for us to be merciful.

Matthew 5: 8 – Blessed are the pure in heart: for they shall see God.

Non-believers, and others who are worldly, scoff at the pure in heart, considering them to be foolish, naïve, out of touch with reality, etc., but to Jesus they are the true realists. They view the world thru a prism of spiritual reality, striving to reject the false gods of this world in favor of the one true God.

Over and over again we read in the Scriptures how Jesus strives to make it clear that our physical lives are temporary in nature. And over and over again, (with every breath we take) Jesus provides us with the opportunity of finding Him, and traveling His way to eternal salvation.

To be pure in heart is to be possessed of the insight, that the values of this world created by Satan, are as cold water splashed on a hot rock; appearing substantive, but soon to disappear into a steam of nothingness. Those who are pure in heart believe in, and love Jesus unquestioningly. They live their lives in the sure knowledge that they will see Jesus in the world to come. The Holy Spirit has entered their lives, and blessed them with spiritual knowledge resulting in certainty of behavior that will ultimately result in righteousness of character sufficient to qualify as God's companions in paradise.

Matthew 5: 9 – Blessed are the peacemakers: for they shall be called the children of God.

Oftentimes those who seek to settle differences, or break up a fight, or offer themselves as intermediaries are criticized, ostracized, scorned, abused, and sometimes murdered for their efforts. The reward for a peacemaker is not in this world, but in the next where he will enjoy a child/parent relationship with God.

It takes extraordinary moral strength, and trust in God's will to be a peacemaker, and to attain all the states of blessedness expressed in the Beatitudes, but the reward is great.

Perhaps no other commandment separates those who love Jesus from those who only profess to love Him. From personal levels of disagreements, escalating all the way up to worldwide disputes, the overwhelming modus operandi for dealing with disagreements has been belligerent self-interest, ultimately leading to confrontation, threats of war, and actual wars.

These problems are amenable to solution on an individual basis, one person at a time opting to follow Jesus. This means expressing sincere sorrow for sinful behavior, renouncing Satan, and rejecting the tired, disproved formulas for solving disputes in favor of obeying the codes generated by the Beatitudes, and all the other codes proclaimed by Jesus.

The Holy Spirit abiding in us makes it possible to obey the Beatitudes, and all the codes required to attain heaven on earth now, and in the world to come.

<u>Matthew 5: 10-12</u> - Blessed are they which are persecuted for righteousness' sake: for theirs is the kingdom of heaven.

Blessed are ye, when men shall revile you, and persecute you, and shall say all manner of evil against you falsely, for my sake.

Rejoice, and be exceeding glad: for great is your reward in heaven: for so persecuted they the prophets which were before you.

Believers in Christ do not be deceived! You will be persecuted for living your faith. Numerous verses of Scripture attest to this fact. Persecution can take the form of subtle discrimination such as exclusion from a group, looks of derision cast your way, etc., or you may suffer less subtle, more direct and/or severe forms of persecution. Regardless of the type or severity of the victimization you suffer, have no doubt that it will happen. The following verses affirm the reality of persecution, and the certainty of its' infliction on those who love Jesus, and attempt to live accordingly:

2 Timothy 3: 12 – "Yea, and all that live Godly in Christ shall suffer persecution."

*Acts 5: 41 – "And they departed from the presence of the council, rejoicing that they were counted worthy to suffer shame for his name." * *

*The apostles had defied the ruling of the high priest that they should not teach in the name of Jesus. As a result, they were beaten and then let go.

Acts 7: 52 – "Which of the prophets have not your fathers persecuted? and they have slain them which showed before of *the coming of the Just One; of whom ye have been now the betrayers and murderers:" **

* - Stephen spoke these words and other words of rebuke directed against the leaders of the Jewish High Council. As a result, he was stoned to death and became the first martyr of the early Christian church.

In his first general Epistle, Peter directed the following remarks to those Jewish believers who were suffering persecution:

1Peter 4: 12 – "Beloved, think it not strange concerning the fiery trial which is to try you, as though some strange thing happened unto you."

It takes extraordinary moral strength, and trust in God's will to suffer persecution for Christ's' sake, and to attain all the states of blessedness expressed in the Beatitudes, but the rewards are great.

The Holy Spirit abiding in us makes it possible to obey the Beatitudes, and all the codes required to attain heaven on earth now, and in the world to come.

The daily recitation of the Beatitudes (conditions of blessedness proclaimed by Jesus) is an excellent way to remind us of Jesus and His teachings. They are repeated below for quick reference:

Matthew 5: 3-12:

1. - Blessed are the poor in spirit: for theirs is the kingdom of heaven.

2. – Blessed are they that mourn: for they shall be comforted.

3. – Blessed are the meek: for they shall inherit the earth.

4. – Blessed are they which do hunger and thirst after righteousness: for they shall be filled.

5 – Blessed are the merciful: for they shall obtain mercy.

6. – Blessed are the pure in heart: for they shall see God.

7. – Blessed are the peacemakers: for they shall be called the children of God.

8. – Blessed are they which are persecuted for righteousness' sake: for theirs is the kingdom of heaven.

Blessed are ye when men shall revile you, and persecute you, and shall say all manner of evil against you falsely, for my sake.

Rejoice, and be exceeding glad: for so persecuted they the prophets which were before you.

So ends the first of the two segments added to Chapter twenty-three. The first additional segment dealt with the Beatitudes. The second additional segment, which follows below, deals with the first man and woman, Adam and Eve, and with the relationships involving the genders, male and female.

it is safe to say that we are in urgent need of a 'Hosea'. But more importantly, we need to listen to the word of God, believe in Jesus, obey His commands and love Jesus, the one who loves us more than is humanly possible.

<u>Adam and Eve</u>

Some readers of the Bible contend that homosexuality is a sin against God, and that our political leaders and other social elites applaud it. They contend that these luminaries seek to obliterate or at least blur the distinctions between male and female, distinctions originally determined and declared by our Creator God.

However we might agree or disagree with their contention, as regards Adam and Eve, most believers acknowledge that God first created man out of the dust of the ground, and from the rib of the man, God made the woman.

The verses presented below offer an overview of the biblical attitude regarding homosexuality, same sex marriages and other forms of sexual activities and conditions removed from established Biblical norms:

<u>*Genesis 1: 26-28*</u> *–"– "And God said, Let us make man in our image, after our likeness: and let them have dominion over the fish of the sea, and over the fowl of the air, and over the cattle, and over all the earth, and over every creeping thing that creepeth upon the earth.*

So God created man, in his own image, in the image of God created he him; male and female created he them.

And God blessed them, and God said unto them, Be fruitful and multiply, and replenish the earth, and subdue it: and have dominion over the fish of the sea, and over the fowl of the air, and over every living thing that moveth upon the earth."

Genesis 1: 29 – "And God said, Behold, I have given you every herb bearing seed which is upon the face of all the earth, and every tree, in the which is the fruit of a tree yielding seed; to you it shall be for meat."

Genesis 2: 7 – "And the Lord God formed man of the dust of the ground and breathed into his nostrils the breath of life; and man became a living soul.

Genesis 2: 8 – "And the Lord God planted a garden eastward in Eden; and there he put the man whom he had formed."

Genesis 2: 18 – "And the Lord God said, it is not good that the man should be alone; I will make him an help meet for him."

<u>*Genesis 2: 21-23 -*</u>

Genesis 2: 21 - "And the Lord God caused a deep sleep to fall upon Adam, and he slept: and he took one of his ribs, and closed up the flesh instead thereof;"

Genesis 2: 22 - And the rib, which the Lord God had taken from man, made he a woman, and brought her unto the man.

Genesis 2: 23 - And Adam said, This is now bone of my bones, and flesh of my flesh: she shall be called Woman, because she was taken out of Man."

Genesis 2: 24 – "Therefore * shall a man leave his father and his mother, and shall cleave unto his wife: and they shall be one flesh."

* - The word "Therefore" indicates that it is Adam who is speaking following the words he spoke in Genesis 2: 23, but that is not the case.

As recorded in the Gospel according to Matthew, Chapter 19, verses 4-6, Jesus, while responding to a question put to him by the Pharisees, clearly indicates that God - *("... he which made them at the beginning ....")* - spoke the words recorded in Genesis 2: 24.

Matthew 19: 4,5,6

Matthew 19: 4 - "And he answered and said unto them,

Have ye not read, that he which made them at the beginning made them male and female,"

* - (Here, Jesus repeats and reaffirms the essence of the message spoken by God as recorded in Genesis 1: 27.

Matthew 19: 5 – "And said, For this cause shall a man leave father and mother, and shall cleave to his wife: and they twain be one flesh?" *

* - Here Jesus repeats and reaffirms the essence of the message spoken by God as recorded in Genesis 2: 24.

Matthew 19: 6 – "Wherefore they are no more twain, but one flesh." * *What God therefore hath joined together let not man put asunder."*

* - Here again Jesus repeats and reaffirms the essence of the message spoken by God as recorded in Genesis 2: 24.

The second sentence – *"What God therefore hath joined together, let not man put asunder"* constitutes an additional lesson regarding the importance of marriage in the eyes of God. It is only as recorded here in Matthew 19: 6, and in Mark 10: 9 that Jesus' uses the word "asunder" in connection with the sanctity of marriage and the importance of keeping it from being torn apart.

Let's attempt to provide some random commentary regarding the essential contents of the verses presented above dealing with the creation of Adam and Eve, and God's plans for them:

God created humankind and gave him dominion over all the earth and over all its non-human inhabitants.

God created man and woman to look like him and to be like him.

God blessed Adam and Eve and told them to replenish the earth. In order to comply with this command, the only means available to them was via sexual intercourse. None of the modern day scientific innovations devised to promote, assist and encourage intercourse, conception and successful births had yet been developed.

Nevertheless Adam and Eve and their progeny were highly successful in carrying out the Lords command to replenish the earth.

God's command to "replenish" the earth, rather than to populate it, appears to indicate that the earth had, at some point in time before Adam and Eve, been populated. And since Adam and Eve would only be able to produce human offspring, in their efforts to comply with God's command to replenish the earth, we can conclude that the earth had formerly been populated by humans.

Who were these people? When were these people? Why were these people? If the answer is that no such people ever existed, then the use of the word "replenish" by Moses (believed to be the author of the first five books of the Bible) was used carelessly or inadvertently. Most lovers of sacred scripture are not prepared to accept the idea of the careless use of a word by Moses.

Suffice it to say, the Bible does not provide any additional information regarding this matter.

Adam and Eve had available to them for food only the fruits and vegetables produced by plant life. Therefore, prior to the flood, human kind was vegetarian.

When God created Adam out of the dust of the ground, he breathed into Adam's nostrils the breath of life, and Adam became a living soul. Adam became physically and spiritually alive, unique of all earth's creatures, made in the image and likeness of God.

The implication is that unless Adam had a companion, he would be lonely and unhappy. God decided that a companion for Adam would be best qualified by a person like him, one who compliments Adam's attributes.

Whether or not the removal of Adam's rib was painful, sacred scripture does not say. What we do know is that God caused Adam to be in deep sleep when his rib was removed and the wound was closed. And because there is also no indication in the scripture of after-surgery pain, we can assume that there was none. The apparent valid conclusion is that Adam did not suffer pain during or after the procedure.

God allowed Adam to name the newly created human, and because she was made from Adam's God-created body, Adam called her "woman", the transliteration of the Hebrew word which means, "the other part of man".

When a man marries a woman, he is no longer a person alone; the woman he marries becomes a living part of him.

But what additionally does the Bible have to say regarding human sexual relationships as they relate to the creation narrative regarding Adam and Eve, and as they relate to their progeny? The following verses provide some information in answer to that question:

Jude, half-brother to Jesus authored a general epistle (consisting of one Chapter containing 25 verses) mostly dedicated to the dangers of false prophets, how to combat their evil doctrines, and Jude's urgent exhortations to remain true to Jesus Christ.

Jude 8 – "Likewise also these filthy dreamers defile the flesh, despise dominion, and speak evil of dignitaries." *

* - Speaking against those whom he believes are apostate teachers, Jude first and foremost categorizes them as "filthy dreamers".

The word "filthy" carries with it the connotation of sexual deviancy of a homosexual nature. Whether or not they all are filthy in that sense might depend on an individual evaluation of each one, but the fact that they are called dreamers indicates that they do not face reality; they propose solutions and promote causes without proper consideration of the facts of life. They talk big but produce small.

Next Jude accuses these dreamers of defiling the flesh. This is language similar in tone to that used to describe the behavior of the inhabitants of Sodom and Gomorrah in the Old Testament wherein they defiled the flesh.

These filthy dreamers, defile the flesh, reject legally constituted authority, and encourage hatred of prominent persons in and out of government.

Asa king of Judah, (circa 910-869) does the right thing in the eyes of the Lord:

I Kings 15: 12 – "And he took away the sodomites out of the land, and removed all the idols that his fathers had made." *

* - Rampant sodomy evidently went hand in hand with idol worship during the time frame of Genesis –(the first book of the Bible), and during the time frame of Jude –(the next to last book of the Bible.)

In the latter years of John the apostle's life, he penned his Epistles whose purpose was to comfort and strengthen the faith of believers and to counteract the teachings of the Gnostics who taught that knowledge of God was the means to salvation, rather than Jesus' sacrifice on the cross.

*1 John 3: 9 – "Whosoever is born of God doth not commit sin; for his seed remaineth in him: and he cannot sin, because he is born of God." ***

* - These words by John are meant to be encouraging rather than a condemnation of us all. They are a reminder that God within us has the power to make it so that there is no room for sin in our spiritual life; no room for our sinning self.

The Holy Spirit has the power to strengthen our resolve to sin no more. None are perfect except He who came to pay the debt of our sins. Jesus will never give up on those who fall into sin, but then struggle to get up again to fight the good fight.

God can deliver the power to escape from a sinful life.

As recorded in the book of Genesis, Lot offers hospitality to two strangers at his home in Sodom:

<u>*Genesis 19: 4-5*</u>

"But before they lay down, the men of the city, even Sodom, compassed the house round, both old and young, all the people from every quarter:

*And they called unto Lot, and said unto him, Where are the men which came into thee this night? Bring them out unto us, that we may know them." ***

* - To *"know them"* as spoken by the men of Sodom was intended to convey the sexual connotation of sodomizing the two guests of Lot.

Unknown to Lot and to the townspeople of Sodom, the two strangers to whom Lot offered hospitality were angels of God. Not only does God know all that we do, sometimes an angel of God might be with you. But not only that; If you believe in Jesus and make room for the Holy Spirit, God can be with you, always.

What a wonderful thought – to have God always with you. Not so wonderful for determined sinners to realize that every thought, word and deed is known to our Father in heaven.

The Old Testament book of Leviticus is the third book of the bible, written by Moses as made known to him by God.

*Leviticus 18: 22 – "Thou shalt not lie with mankind as with womankind: it is abomination. ***

* - Same gender sexual activities are an abomination to God.

Just a short while before his martyrdom Peter penned his second epistle. In it he attempted to fortify his readers against the teachings of the false prophets who were sure to follow his demise.

2 Peter 2: 4 – "For if God spared not the angels that sinned, but cast them into chains of darkness, to be reserved unto judgment.

2 Peter 2: 6 – "And turning the cities of Sodom and Gomorrah into ashes condemned them with an overthrow making them an example unto those that after should live ungodly;"

* - No status, not that of an angel or that of a disciple is above God's righteous judgment.

Although as believers in Jesus we no longer labor under the burden of living under the Law of the Old Testament, the Bible, both in the Old and the New Testaments make it abundantly clear that homosexual behavior is forbidden by God.

By strongly supporting the Law and the prophets of the Old Testament, Jesus confirms God's desire for the propagation of the human race via male and female physical intercourse, preferably accomplished in a traditional marriage as established in the Old Testament, but he does not belabor the point.

In sum and substance, the Sermon on the Mount embodies the states of blessedness deemed praise worthy by God. But in the Beatitudes Jesus does not make mention of homosexual behavior as being an impediment to attaining a state of blessedness. Nor in the Gospels or in the remainder of the New Testament does Jesus comment regarding homosexuality.

Personally and in accordance with the Scriptures, I do not approve of gay marriage, homosexual activity and the like, but deep down I know it is not right to dislike, look down on, or condemn those who are that way. I am certain that Jesus Christ, the perfect man and perfect God loves all of us more than is humanly possible, and that his promise of salvation to all those who believe in him and repent of their sins, excludes no class of people.

The command to Adam, and Eve to go forth and replenish the earth was made by God to those two, both of whom were physically, and emotionally capable of reproducing in the manner God established, that is to say, one man and one woman, bound together as one flesh. And by a vast majority, the progeny of Adam and Eve were also well equipped to carry out God's command to replenish the earth. But over the millennia, as the populations increased, so too did that of those who are not physically, and/or emotionally capable of procreating in accordance with acceptable biblical standards. These people are, as are all of humankind, created in the image and likeness of God.

Thus ends the two segments added to Chapter Twenty-three.

Notes and Reflections

_____
_____
_____
_____
_____
_____
_____
_____
_____
_____
_____
_____
_____
_____
_____
_____
_____
_____
_____
_____
_____
_____
_____
_____
_____
_____
_____
_____
_____
_____

Chapter Twenty-Four

Significant trumpet associations derived from the book of Joel:

Joel was a contemporary of the prophet Hosea, but resided in Jerusalem and was therefore known as a prophet of the southern kingdom. The book of Joel is short, containing only three chapters, but is unique in that he repeatedly calls for Judah to prepare for the day of the Lord. Joel refers not only, short-range to the plague of locusts which has left their cupboards bare coupled with the threat of more attacks on the horizon, but even more importantly Joel speaks of the second coming of Jesus beginning with the Rapture of his church, after which He will pronounce righteous judgment upon the living and the dead.

Joel 1: 15 – "Alas for the day! For the day of the Lord is at hand, and as a destruction from the Almighty shall it come."

Joel 2: 1 – "Blow ye the <u>trumpet</u> in Zion, and sound an alarm in my holy mountain: let all the inhabitants of the land tremble: for the day of the Lord cometh, for it is nigh at hand;"

2: 15 – "Blow the <u>trumpet</u> in Zion, sanctify a fast, call a solemn assembly:"

(sta) 91. – During a time of great strife in Judah, Joel the prophet called for the trumpet to blare a warning of forthcoming invasions.

(sta) 92. - And again during a time of great strife in Judah, Joel called for the trumpet to blare as a call to gather in solemn assembly for the purpose of promoting a rededication to the Lord God of creation, and to possibly illuminate the people regarding Joel's prophecy regarding the reality of the Son of God, the Rapture of his church, and of his righteous judgment upon the living and the dead.

And so ends Chapter Twenty-four.

Chapter Twenty-four yields two significant trumpet associations:

(sta) 91. – During a time of great strife in Judah, Joel the prophet called for the trumpet to blare a warning of forthcoming invasions.

(sta) 92. - And again during a time of great strife in Judah, Joel called for the trumpet to blare, this time as a call to gather in solemn assembly for the purpose of promoting a rededication to the Lord God of Creation, and to possibly illuminate the people regarding Joel's prophecy regarding the reality of the Son of God, the Rapture of his church, and of his righteous judgment upon the living and the dead.

Notes and Reflections

_____
_____
_____
_____
_____
_____
_____
_____
_____
_____
_____
_____
_____
_____
_____
_____
_____
_____
_____
_____
_____
_____
_____
_____
_____
_____
_____
_____

Chapter Twenty-Five

Significant trumpet associations derived from the book of Amos:

Amos was a contemporary of Hosea. Although born in the southern kingdom of

Judah, he was a prophet to the northern kingdom of Israel. He speaks of the righteous judgment of God concerning Moab during and following the Moabites victory over the Edomites. Moab had killed the king of Edom and had even gone so far as to burn the king's bones, turning them into lime.

Such a despicable act of vengeance against a foe fell far short of acceptable, dismissing out of hand God's clearly stated attitude against usurping His responsibility and power to exact righteous vengeance:

Deuteronomy 32: 35 – "To me belongeth vengeance, and recompense; …."

Romans 12: 19 – "Dearly beloved, avenge not yourselves, but rather give place unto wrath: for it is written, Vengeance is mine; I will repay, saith the Lord."

Amos 2: 2 – "But I will send a fire upon Moab, and it shall devour the palaces of Kirioth: and Moab shall die with tumult, with shouting, and with the sound of the <u>trumpet</u>:"

(sta) 93. – Because of Moab's intransigence, desecrating the body of the king of Edom, exacting personal vengeance, and thereby usurping the authority and power of God, Moab pays with his life.

Amos 2: 3 – "And I will cut off the judge from the midst thereof, and will slay all the princes thereof with him, saith the Lord.

(sta) 94. - As further evidence of God's displeasure with Edom, not only is the king killed, but so also are all the princes! This spells the end of Edom, forever.

Amos 3: 6 – "Shall a <u>trumpet</u> be blown in the city, and the people not be afraid? Shall there be evil in a city and the Lord hath not done it?

Thru Amos, God asks a rhetorical question: If a warning trumpet sound should the people be afraid?

Well of course they should be afraid: afraid enough to convince them to obey the Lord's commandments and to worship only Him only as the one true God, but incredibly they do not comply.

If evil flourishes, is it happening because God does not know what is going on? Of course not. Evil flourishes all around them, because as God's chosen people, more is expected of them. But unfortunately, idolatry, lusts of the flesh, other worldly cravings, and just plain stubbornness carries the day.

(sta) 95. — Sometimes not even God's warning trumpet is enough to convince sinners to repent.

And so ends Chapter Twenty-five.

Chapter Twenty-five yields three significant trumpet associations:

(sta) 93. — Because of Moab's intransigence, desecrating the body of the king of Edom, exacting personal vengeance, and thereby usurping the authority and power of God, Moab pays with his life.

(sta) 94. - As further evidence of God's displeasure with Edom, not only is the king killed, but so also are all the princes! This spells the end of Edom, forever.

(sta) 95. — Sometimes not even God's warning trumpet is enough to convince sinners to repent.

Notes and Reflections

Chapter Twenty-Six

Significant trumpet associations derived from the book of Zephaniah:

The word of God comes to the minor prophet Zephaniah at approximately 620 B.C.

He exhorts Judah to seek out the Lord, and to turn away from their idolatrous practices before the Lord's Day of judgment.

In my inner spirit, I hear Zephaniah's sad but resolute voice as he speaks to Judah: "Yes Judah, you had your way, but now it is time to pay."

I hesitate to listen too closely. I fear those same words will now speak to us, speak to our beautiful country. Please Heavenly Father, give us, give all of us, just one more chance.

Now is the time: Repent, pray, love your neighbor as yourself, love Jesus, and allow the Holy Spirit to abide in you.

Zephaniah 1: 16 – "A day of the trumpet and alarm against the fenced cities, and against the high towers."

(sta) 96. - The day of warning and of war against the fortified cities is at hand. There is no place to hide, no port secure from the oncoming storm. The only safe harbor is that which you decided to pass by - the love and worship of the one true God. Instead you chose the trumpet of war over the love of the Almighty, and you chose the wanton fierceness of God's surrogates over the mercy and forgiveness He repeatedly implored you to accept.

And so ends Chapter Twenty-six.

Chapter Twenty-six yields one significant trumpet association:

(sta) 96. - The day of warning and of war against the fortified cities is at hand. There is no place to hide, no port secure from the oncoming storm. The only safe harbor is that which you decided to pass by - the love and worship of the one true God. Instead you chose the trumpet of war over the love of the Almighty, and you chose the wanton fierceness of God's surrogates over the mercy and forgiveness He repeatedly implored you to accept.

Notes and Reflections

Chapter Twenty-Seven

Significant trumpet associations derived from the book of Zechariah:

Zechariah's prophecies offered words of encouragement to the retuning exiles of which he was one. He urged the rebuilding of the temple and a rededication to the Lord.

Zechariah 9: 14 – *"And the Lord shall be seen over them, and his arrow shall go forth as the lightning: and the Lord God shall blow the <u>trumpet</u>; and shall go with whirlwinds of the south."*

(sta) 97. - Herein is the promise of the Lord, that the Lord will be Israel's champion in battle, that the Lord will blow the trumpet of certain victory over the enemies of the remnant of His chosen people.

And so ends Chapter Twenty-seven.

Chapter Twenty-seven yields one significant trumpet association:

(sta) 97. - Herein is the promise of the Lord, that the Lord will be Israel's champion in battle, that the Lord will blow the trumpet of certain victory over the enemies of the remnant of His chosen people.

Notes and Reflections

Chapter Twenty-Eight

Significant trumpet associations derived from the Gospel according to Matthew:

The words of Jesus as he continues to instruct His disciples and future believers on the proper ways to lead a life of Christ:

Matthew 6: 2 - "Therefore when thou doest thine alms, do not sound a trumpet before thee, as the hypocrites do in the synagogues and in the streets, that they may have glory of men. Verily I say unto you, They have their reward."

(sta) 98. - One of Jesus' pet peeves was hypocrisy, a highly developed characteristic of Israel's religious elite as exemplified by the Pharisees and the temple priests. Often times their religious fervor and ostentatious adoration of God were nothing more than ("Look at me, aren't I wonderful?") attention seeking ploys.

In other words, Jesus tells His disciples, When you pray don't announce yourself with blaring trumpets; instead, reach out to the Lord your creator with unfeigned fervor, deeply grateful for all the gifts He has bestowed on you and on all of mankind (sta) 99. - If what you seek is the recognition, praise and approval of your fellow man, rather than God's love and gift of eternal salvation, then rest easy:

Simply, blow your own trumpet, - (the louder the better)

Ride the tide of popular opinion.

Be still when your Christian faith is shaken and under attack.

Make sure to abandon the standards of decency, mercy and love you embraced as a child, but which somehow loosed from your grasp as time moved along.

(sta) 100. - The freedom and ability to pray is another precious gift from God. Use it often and well. No trumpet needed.

Within the confines of your inner spirit, seek to bare your soul to the God that made you.

Matthew 24: 31 – "And he shall send his angels with a great sound of a trumpet, and they shall gather together his elect from the four winds, from one end of heaven to the other."

Matthew 24: 31 speaks not of when Christ first returns to fulfill the Rapture of His church, but rather of His return to earth near the end of the Great Tribulation. At that time, accompanied by a trumpet blare of unimaginable decibels, Jesus will command his angels to gather the dispersed of Israel, the remnant of Jewry – 144 thousand Jews. It is then that the Jews will repent of their sins, acknowledge Jesus as their true Messiah, and become in active reality, as well as in sacred Scripture, "God's Chosen People."

And so ends Chapter Twenty-eight.

Chapter Twenty-eight yields three significant trumpet associations:

(sta) 98. - One of Jesus' pet peeves was hypocrisy, a highly developed characteristic of Israel's religious elite as exemplified by the Pharisees and the temple priests. Often times their religious fervor and ostentatious adoration of God were nothing more than ("Look at me, aren't I wonderful?") attention seeking ploys.

In other words, Jesus tells His disciples, When you pray don't announce yourself with blaring trumpets; instead, reach out to the Lord your creator with unfeigned fervor, deeply grateful for all the gifts He has bestowed on you and on all of mankind

(sta) 99. - If what you seek is the recognition, praise and approval of your fellow man, rather than God's love and gift of eternal salvation, then rest easy:

Simply, blow your own trumpet, - (the louder the better)

Ride the tide of popular opinion.

Be still when your Christian faith is shaken and under attack.

Make sure to abandon the standards of decency, mercy and love you embraced as a child, but which somehow loosed from your grasp as time moved along.

(sta) 100. - The freedom and ability to pray is another precious gift from God. Use it often and well. No trumpet needed.

Within the confines of your inner spirit, seek to bare your soul to the God that made you.

Notes and Reflections

Chapter Twenty-Nine

Significant trumpet associations derived from the first epistle of Paul to the Corinthians:

Written in approximately A.D. 55, Paul's first epistle to the church he founded at Corinth was prompted by the many questions he had received from the church regarding political, religious, and practical matters. Basically, Paul seeks to remind and reassure the leaders of the church that the answer to all their problems is Jesus Christ. Complete trust and faith in Jesus is the solution, the only solution.

1 Corinthians 14: 8 - "For if the <u>trumpet</u> give an uncertain sound, who shall prepare himself for the battle?" *

* - I am reminded of the words spoken by Jesus as recorded in the Gospel according to Matthew, chapter 5, verse 13:

"Ye are the salt of the earth: but if the salt have lost his savour, wherewith shall it be salted? It is thenceforth good for nothing, but to be cast out, and to be trodden under foot of men.

The sound of the trumpet is unique and specific according to its purpose. The message of the disciples is unique and specific to its purpose.

In either case, the trumpet sound or the disciple's message, any weakness or essential variation in in the manner in which they are conveyed would dilute or distort the intended message.

(sta) -101. - If salt loses its saltiness, what is available to flavor the food? If the trumpet loses its proper blare, what is available to sound the alarm?

The Gospels are the Word of God. The trumpet is God's emergency alert. They are both instruments chosen to foster His will.

Also in Paul's first letter to the Corinthians he spells out in goodly detail the Resurrection narrative of Jesus, and the resurrection to come of those believers who have gone to their rest awaiting His return.

1 Corinthians 15: 52 – "In a moment, in the twinkling of an eye, at the last <u>trump</u>: for the trumpet shall sound, and the dead shall be raised incorruptible, and we shall be changed."*

* - I Corinthians 15: 52 speaks of when Jesus next returns on the clouds of heaven, accompanied by the trumpets blare to" Rapture" his church. Those who have gone to their rest in hope of rising again, and those who are living at the time of his return will return with Jesus to the Father in heaven.

(sta) –102. – The "last trump" is the voice of God, His last call to all believers: Come! Join him in eternal peace and happiness. Come! Your reward is great for staying the course. Come! Jesus God, Creator of heaven and earth loves you more than is humanly possible. Come! Bid farewell to the

worries of this world. Say hello to your new, incorruptible body. Come! Jesus of Nazareth has prepared a place for you in the kingdom of God.

And so ends Chapter Twenty-nine.

Chapter Twenty-nine yields two significant trumpet associations:

(sta) -101. - If salt loses its saltiness, what is available to flavor the food? If the trumpet loses its proper blare, what is available to sound the alarm?

The Gospels are the Word of God. The trumpet is God's emergency alert. They are both instruments chosen to foster His will.

(sta) – 102. – The "last trump" is the voice of God, His last call to all believers: Come! Join him in eternal peace and happiness. Come! Your reward is great for staying the course. Come! Jesus God, Creator of heaven and earth loves you more than is humanly possible. Come! Bid farewell to the worries of this world. Say hello to your new, incorruptible body. Come! Jesus of Nazareth has prepared a place for you in the kingdom of God.

Notes and Reflections

Chapter Thirty

Significant trumpet associations derived from 1 Thessalonians:

1 Thessalonians 4: 16, 17 *

4: 16 - "For the Lord himself shall descend from the heaven with a shout, with the voice of the archangel, and with the trump of God: and the dead in Christ shall rise first."

4: 17 – "Then we which are alive and remain shall be caught up together with them in the clouds, to meet the Lord in the air: and so shall we ever be with the Lord."

* - Paul's first Epistle to the Corinthians, Chapter 4, verses 16-17 ^, was previously mentioned in chapter Eleven of this book, and yielded (Sta) 45 as indicated below:

"When next Jesus comes again, the trumpet sound will signal the initiation of the transformation from corruptible physical bodies to incorruptible spiritual ones, both for the living and for the dead."

And so ends Chapter Thirty

Chapter Thirty yields no significant trumpet associations, but serves as a reminder of, and provides supporting scripture for (sta) 45. as formulated earlier in Chapter eleven:

"When next Jesus comes again, the trumpet sound will signal the initiation of the transformation from corruptible physical bodies to incorruptible spiritual ones, both for the living, and for the dead in Christ."

Notes and Reflections

Chapter Thirty-One

Significant trumpet associations derived from the New Testament book - "The Epistle to the Hebrews":

Hebrews 12: 18-21

12: 18 - "For ye are not come unto the mount that might be touched, and that burned with fire, nor unto blackness, and darkness, and tempest."

12: 19 – "And the sound of a <u>trumpet</u>, and the voice of words; which voice they that heard entreated that the word should not be spoken to them any more:"

12: 20 – ("For they could not endure that which was commanded, And if so much as a beast touch the mountain, it shall be stoned, or thrust through with a dart:"

12: 21 – "And so terrible was the sight, that Moses said, I exceedingly fear and quake:)"

The above quoted words refer to the time in the Old Testament when Moses received the Law directly from God on Mount Sinai. At that time, as recorded in Exodus 32: 28, three thousand people were slain as a judgment against the Hebrew idolaters.

These remarks by Paul to the Hebrews were a reminder to those Jews who had come to Christ, (and as a result were shunned and ostracized by the rest of Judaism) that their suffering as believers in Christ Jesus, was light compared to that of the sons of Levi who were commanded to slay those Hebrews who remained steadfast in their worship of false gods and their continued rejection of their Creator, the one true God.

(sta) 103. – The trumpet sound combined with the terrible punishment commanded by Moses against the idol-worshipers at Mount Sinai in the Old Testament reflect God's deadly judgments inherent in the Old Covenant, as contrasted with the three thousand Jews who came to Christ as recorded in the New Testament book – "The Acts Of The Apostles", chapter two, verse 41. – "Then they that gladly received his word were baptized: and the same day there were added unto them about three thousand souls."

Three thousand souls lost to God the Father, via idolatry in the Old Testament are juxtaposed in (sta) 103. with the three thousand souls won to God the Son, by Peter, imbued with the Holy Spirit in the New.

Approximately sixteen hundred years separate these two episodes of divine intentions as manifested by Moses on one hand, and by Peter on the other. But as we ruminate and contemplate on God's judgments, decisions, and plans, sacred Scripture reveals that they – (God's judgments, decision, and plans) - are not impacted by the passage of time, or the opinions of men.

And so ends Chapter Thirty-one

Chapter Thirty-one yields one significant trumpet association:

(sta) 103. – The trumpet sound combined with the terrible punishment commanded by Moses against the idol-worshipers at Mount Sinai in the Old Testament reflect God's deadly judgments inherent in the Old Covenant, as contrasted with the three thousand Jews who came to Christ as recorded in the New Testament book – "The Acts Of The Apostles", chapter two, verse 41. – "Then they that gladly received his word were baptized: and the same day there were added unto them about three thousand souls."

Notes and Reflections

Chapter Thirty-Two

Significant trumpet associations derived from the book of Revelation:

The book of Revelation is the final book of the Bible. It contains information revealed to John by Jesus the Resurrected Christ, while John was living in exile on the island of Patmos. One part of the Revelation deals with information concerning seven churches located in Asia Minor. The second part relates to the end times of this age, (the Church age) and to the events and ages that follow it.

Although ample use is made of symbols and symbolism, the book of Revelation, whether by use of symbols or by direct language, relates entirely to reality, whether of the past, the present, or the future.

Revelation 1:10; 4: 1; 8: 2, 6, 13

Revelation 1: 10 – "I was in the spirit on the Lord's day, and heard behind me a great voice, as of a trumpet,"

When John heard these words, and all the other words directed to him as recorded in the book of Revelation, he was under the direct influence of God the Holy Spirit. He compares the very first instance of Christ's revelation to him as sounding like the great voice of a trumpet.

(sta) 104. – Both in the Old and in the New Testaments, God's favored instrument of choice is the trumpet.

Revelation 4: 1 – "After this I looked, and, behold, a door was opened in heaven: and the first voice which I heard was as it were of a <u>trumpet</u> talking with me; which said, Come up hither, and I will show thee things which must be hereafter."

To say, "set in concrete" would not be strong enough to describe the absolute certainty that the things spoken of following verse 4: 1 will happen because they are to be revealed by the Holy Spirit while John remains in the Spirit.

(sta) 105. –Whether portrayed in divine visions purposed to communicate reality, or in instances reflecting direct reality, the trumpet's trump is fashioned and utilized by God to inform and facilitate the carrying out of His divine will.

Revelation 8: 2 – "And I saw the seven angels which stood before God; and to them were given seven <u>trumpets</u>."

Revelation 8: 6 – "And the seven angels which had the seven <u>trumpets</u> prepared themselves to sound."

(Sta)106. - Seven angels chosen by God will be prepared to sound trumps of coming destructions; the first four of which are intended to convince the as-yet unrepentant to repent before the final three trumpets of destruction sound.

What follows now are the verses of Revelation that refer to the first four trumpets, what they portend, what they describe, and what they bring about. In these verses whenever it states that an angel sounded, it refers to the sounding of the trumpet:

Revelation 8: 7 – "The first angel sounded, and there followed hale and fire mingled with blood, and they were cast upon the earth: and the third part of trees was burnt up, and all green grass was burnt up."

<u>*Revelation 8: 8-9*</u> *– "And the second angel sounded, and as It were a great mountain burning with fire was cast into the sea: and the third part of the sea become blood;*

And the third part of the creatures which were in the sea, and had life, died; and the third part of the ships were destroyed."

<u>*Revelation 8: 10-11*</u> *– "And the third angel sounded, and there fell a great star from heaven, burning as it were a lamp, and it fell upon the third part of the rivers, and upon the fountains of water;*

And the name of the star is called Wormwood: and the third part of the waters became wormwood; and many men died of the waters, because they were made bitter."

Revelation 8: 12 – "And the fourth angel sounded, and the third part of the sun was smitten, and the third part of the moon, and the third part of the stars; so as the third part of them was darkened, and the day shone not for a third part of It, and the night likewise."

Revelation 8: 13 - "And I beheld, and heard an angel flying through the midst of heaven, saying with a loud voice, Woe, woe, woe, to the inhabiters of the earth by reason of the other voices of the <u>trumpet</u> of the three angels, which are yet to sound."

* - Now, as though things were not already deadly serious enough, the mounting troubles associated with God's judgments are fast coming to a head.

(sta) 107. - An angel of the Lord, flying righteous and true in the very midst of heaven proclaims triple woe to the remaining inhabitants of the earth. Those who have not met Jesus in the descending clouds of heaven when he raptured his church, or have otherwise failed to repent and accept Jesus of Nazareth as their Lord and Savior will now be subject to the final three, the saddest, most frightening trumpets of God.

What next follows are the verses dealing with the sounding of the final three of the aforementioned seven trumpets

<u>*Revelation 9: 1-12*</u> *– "And the fifth angel sounded, and I saw a star fall from heaven unto the earth: and to him was given the key of the bottomless pit.*

And he opened the bottomless pit; and there arose a smoke out of the pit, as the smoke of a great furnace; and the sun and the air were darkened by reason of the smoke of the pit.

And there came out of the smoke locusts upon the earth; and unto them was given power as the scorpions of the earth have power.

And it was commanded them that they should not hurt the grass of the earth, neither any green thing, neither any tree; but only those men which have not the seal of God in their foreheads.

And to them it was given that they should not kill them, but that they should be tormented five months: and their torment was as the torment of a scorpion, when he striketh a man.

And in those days shall men seek death, and shall not find it; and shall desire to die, and death shall flee from them.

And the shapes of the locusts were like unto horses prepared unto battle and on their heads were as it were crowns like gold, and their faces were as the faces of men.

And they had hair as the hair of women, and their teeth were as the teeth of lions.

And they had breastplates, as it were breastplates of iron; and the sound of their wings was as the sound of chariots of many horses running to battle.

And they had tails like unto scorpions, and there were stings in their tails; and their power was to hurt men for five months.

And they had a king over them, which is the angel of the bottomless pit, whose name in the hebrew tongue is Abaddon, but in the Greek tongue hath his name Apolyon.

One woe is past; and, behold, there come two woes more hereafter Revelation 9: 13 – "And the sixth angel sounded, and I heard a voice from the four horns of the golden altar which is before God,

Revelation 9: 14 - Saying to the sixth angel which had the <u>trumpet</u>, Loose the four angels which are bound in the great river Euphrates.

(sta) 108. - The four angels bound in the Euphrates, and loosed by the trumpet sound of the sixth angel are demonic, chosen and prepared by God to direct an army of demons in carrying out punishments and destructions on a terrible scale.

<u>*Revelation 9: 15-21*</u>

And the four angels were loosed, which were prepared for an hour, and a day, and a month, and a year, for to slay the third part of men.

And the number of the army of the horsemen were two hundred thousand thousand: and I heard the number of them.

And thus I saw the horses in the vision, and them that sat on them, having breastplates of fire, and of jacinth, and brimstone: and the heads of the horses were as the heads of lions; and out of their mouths issued fire and smoke and brimstone.

By these three was the third part of men killed, by the fire, and by the smoke, and by the brimstone, which issued out of their mouths.

For their power is in their mouth, and in their tails: for their tails were like unto serpents, and had heads, and with them they do hurt.

And the rest of the men which were not killed by these plagues yet repented not of the works of their hands, that they should not worship devils, and idols of gold, and silver, and brass, and stone, and of wood: which neither can see, nor hear, nor walk.

Neither repented they of their murders, nor of their sorceries, not of their fornication, nor of their thefts."*

* - Incredible as it may seem, there are people who, no matter how awful a price to pay, will not repent of their sins. They wallow in their sins; they worship the false gods of this world; they whole-heartedly reject the Beatitudes, (those eight states of blessedness described by Jesus); they scorn those who attempt to live their lives in accordance with the will of God, and they refuse to acknowledge and accept the mercy, love, and goodness of our God who created them.

It is wonderful comfort to realize that Jesus loves us more than is humanly possible. He wants us to join Him in paradise. He will give us every opportunity to come to Him of our own free will. But, once again, please remember, "God is good, but He is no fool."

Revelation 11: 15 – "And the seventh angel sounded; and there were great voices in heaven saying, The kingdoms of the world are become the kingdoms of our Lord, and of his Christ; and he shall reign for ever and ever."

(sta) 109. – Pronounced by the seventh angel's trumpet-blare, Jesus, the risen Christ righteously assumes kingship over the kingdoms of the world. Jesus the carpenter, the adopted son of a carpenter rules the world.

<u>*Revelation 18: 21-22*</u> *– "And a mighty angel took up a stone like a great millstone, and cast it into the sea, saying, Thus with violence shall that great city Babylon be thrown down and shall be found no more at all.*

And the voices of harpers, and musicians, and of pipers, and <u>trumpeters</u>, shall be heard no more at all in thee; and no craftsman, of whatsoever craft he be, shall be found any more in thee; and the sound of a millstone shall be heard no more at all in thee;"

(sta) 110. –As revealed in Revelation 18: 21-22 the absence of pipers and trumpets tolls the silent death knell - (never to rise again), of the ancient city of Babylon, the capital of the evil Babylonia empire wherein idolatry and paganism flourished.

As revealed in Revelation 18: 21-22, these verses describe how a mighty angel of God proclaims the end of any pleasant and beneficial things that exists in any culture that rejects God. For them, no more the soothing sound of harps, the moving voices of devout singers, or the lively pipes to stir the emotions; all things of the past now, sounds lost to them forever. And gone too, the fine work of craftsmen producing works of beauty and utility, and the comforting grind of millstones, processing grains. And gone too, the trumpet calls to glory, to war, to worship, to assemble, to march or retreat: never to be heard again.

These are the results of God's judgment against peoples, against nations and kingdom, against those who refuse to listen to the truth, against those who worship the gods of this world, against those who lust after power and wealth, against those who wallow in self-pride, and against those who deny to God the glory that is His alone.

And so ends Chapter Thirty-two

Chapter Thirty-two yields seven significant trumpet associations:

(sta) 104. – Both in the Old and in the New Testaments, God's chief instrument of choice is the trumpet.

(sta) 105. –Whether portrayed in divine visions purposed to communicate reality, or in instances reflecting direct reality, the trumpet's trump is fashioned and utilized by God to inform and facilitate the carrying out of His divine will.

(sta)106. - Seven angels chosen by God will be prepared to sound trumps of coming destructions; the first four of which are intended to convince the as-yet unrepentant to repent before the final three trumpets of destruction sound.

(sta) 107. - An angel of the Lord, flying righteous and true in the very midst of heaven proclaims triple woe to the remaining inhabitants of the earth. Those who have not met Jesus in the descending clouds of heaven when he raptured his church, or have otherwise failed to repent and accept Jesus of Nazareth as their Lord and Savior will now be subject to the final three, the saddest, most frightening trumpets of God.

(sta) 108. - *The four angels bound in the Euphrates, and loosed by the trumpet sound of the sixth angel are demonic, chosen and prepared by God to direct an army of demons as they carrying out punishments and destructions on a terrible scale.*

(sta) 109. – *Pronounced by the seventh angel's trumpet-blare, Jesus, the risen Christ righteously assumes kingship over the kingdoms of the world. Jesus the carpenter, the adopted son of a carpenter, rules the world.*

(sta) 110. –*As revealed in Revelation 18: 21-22 the absence of pipers and trumpets tolls the silent death knell - (never to rise again), of the ancient city of Babylon, the capital of the evil Babylonia empire wherein idolatry and paganism flourished.*

Notes and Reflections

Chapter Thirty-Three

Significant trumpet associations derived from a brief study of numbers as they relate to trumpets as derived from the Bible.

It has been proposed that numbers, if properly understood, play an important role in the Bible by being closely associated with particular themes, truths, lessons and commandments. These associations are revealed mostly by dint of repetition, i.e., the same numbers are repeatedly, and/or significantly associated with the same or similar themes, truths, lessons and commandments throughout long periods of biblical history as recorded by numerous scribes who for the most part, had never met, nor communicated with each other.

We will deal with this phenomenon by citing examples as revealed in the Old, and the New Testaments. Any inferences, conclusions, or statements herein provided regarding the relationships that exist between numbers and the Bible are those of yours truly, the author of this book, "Softly Now The Trumpet."

The Old Testament:

The Old Testament of the Bible is made up of 39 Books.

Of these 39 books, twenty-three contain verses wherein one or more of the words, trump, trumpet, trumpeter, and trumpets are mentioned.

In these 23 books the four words combined are mentioned 104 times. Although the number 104 is not found to be significantly associated with particular biblical themes, truths, lessons, and commandments, additional delving into the relationship between the Bible and certain numbers reveals that two of the main components of 104 – (100, and 4) are biblically significant. Therefore these numbers (100 & 4) become our numbers of interest.

By parsing the biblical significance of a number's components, for example, as with the number 104, (the total number of times that our four trumpet words are mentioned in the bible) it provides two component numbers - the numbers 100, and 4, both of which are found to be biblically significant.

These types of trumpet associations are established by mathematical implication rather than by direct mention. For example:

The number of times our trumpet words (trump, trumpets, trumpeter, and trumpets) are mentioned in the bible = 104.

Two components of 104 are found to be biblically significant = 100, and 4.

When biblical themes, truths, lessons, and commandments are specifically linked with these two numbers (100 and

4) in sacred Scripture, then by mathematical implication, so too are trumpets

Genesis, the first book of the Bible serves as the introduction to the next Sixty-five. It establishes the direction of the bible's themes, truths, lessons, and commandments. If Genesis did not exist, there would be no Bible; if the Bible did not exist, we would be ignorant and/or misinformed regarding Creation, and if we were ignorant, or misinformed regarding Creation, our knowledge of our Triune God, God the Father, Son, and Holy Spirit would be distorted, incomplete, or non-existent.

The book of Genesis is, if you will, the theme-setter of the Bible. Therefore when attempting to ascertain Bible/numbers/trumpet relationships established by mathematical implication, the book of Genesis is the primary source of information and validation.

The number 100 is mentioned in the book of Genesis, a total of Sixty-two times.

A selection of these verses is recorded below, highlighting particular themes, truth, lesson, and commandment.

Genesis 5: 3 – "And Adam lived an <u>hundred</u> and thirty years, and begat a son in his own likeness, and after his image; and called his name Seth:"

Genesis 5: 4 – "And the days of Adam after he had begotten Seth were eight <u>hundred</u> years: and he begat sons and daughters:"

229

Genesis 5: 5 – "And all the days that Adam lived were nine <u>hundred</u> and thirty years: and he died.

Based on the verses presented above, the number one hundred is associated with how long lived our earliest ancestors were, compared to our present situation, and with our ancestors ability to produce children in their very old age.

(sta) 111. - By mathematical implication, trumpets are associated with age, longevity, and fertility.

<u>*Genesis 5: 21-24*</u>

5: 21 - "And Enoch lived sixty and five years, and begat Methuselah;"

5: 22 – "And Enoch walked with God after he begat Methuselah three <u>hundred</u> years, and begat sons and daughters."

5: 23 – "And all the days of Enoch were three <u>hundred</u> sixty and five years:

5: 24 – "And Enoch walked with God: and he was not; for God took him." *

* - Enoch did not die. God took him just as he was. Enoch had already proven himself to be a fit companion.

I like to think that when Enoch walked with God on this earth, God held his hand.

My God, I pray: Please hold my hand; let me walk with you.

(sta) – 112 - By mathematical implication, trumpets are associated with a walk with God In this life, followed by an eternal walk with God in the next.

<u>*Genesis 5: 28-29*</u>

28 – "And Lamech lived an <u>hundred</u> eighty and two years, and begat a son:"

5: 29 – "And he called his name Noah, saying, This name shall comfort us concerning our work and toil of our hands, because of the ground which the Lord hath cursed."

(sta) 113. - By mathematical implication trumpets are associated with hope for the future and trust in the Lord.

<u>*Genesis 6: 1-3*</u> *– "And it came to pass, when men began to multiply on the face of the earth, and daughters were born unto them,*

That the sons of God saw the daughters of men that they were fair; and they took them wives of all which they chose.

And the Lord said, My spirit shall not always strive with man, for he also is flesh: yet his days shall be an <u>hundred</u> and twenty years." *

* - The meaning of these verses (Gen. 6: 1-3) is the subject of debate by biblical scholars.

My understanding of them is: God disapproved of the cavalier, supercilious, and self-indulgent manner in which men took to themselves any and all women that appealed to them sexually, without regard to the opinion of the women, their families, or their own families. And as a result of this disapproval, God decided either of two things: One – that the age of men shall be limited to a hundred and twenty years, or Two – that in a hundred and twenty years, God was going to destroy the earth and mankind with it. – (Noah's flood).

The term, "sons of God" was used by God to describe those who believed in Him, in other words, His followers.

The term, "daughters of men" was used by God to describe daughters born to non-believers. God strongly disapproved of believers marrying non-believers, a practice whereby such intermarriages tended to end up in idol worship by 'the sons of god'.

(sta) 114. – By mathematical implication trumpets are associated with God's displeasure with indiscriminate satisfaction of carnal desires by mankind.

(sta) 115. – By mathematical implication trumpets are associated with impending judgment by God.

(sta) 116. – By mathematical implication trumpets are associated with the reduction of mankind's longevity, and/or with God's warning of his intention to destroy some, or all of what He has created.

The remainder of the verses in Genesis that mention 100 and shed light on additional trumpet associations are recorded below.

The Lord begins to give explicit instruction to Noah regarding the measurements of the ark that Noah is instructed by God to build:

Genesis 6: 15 – "And this is the fashion which thou shalt make it of: The length of the ark shall be three hundred cubits, the breadth of it fifty cubits, and the height of it thirty cubits."

(sta) 117. – By mathematical implication trumpets are associated with the process of measuring things, particularly with the process of building the ark.

(sta) 118. – By mathematical implication trumpets are associated with the hope of mankind for salvation, for the rapture of the church, and for eternal reward as companions of God in His kingdom to come.

Genesis 7: 24 – "And the waters prevailed upon the earth an <u>hundred</u> and fifty days."

Genesis 8: 3 – "And the waters returned from off the earth continually: and after the end of the <u>hundred</u> and fifty days the waters were abated.

(sta) 119. - By mathematical implication, trumpets are associated with counting the numbers of things; in particular with how many days the waters of Noah's flood remained fully on the earth, and how many days it took for the waters to completely drain off.

Whilst Abram is in a deep sleep, God speaks to him, telling him that the Hebrew people will be subjugated by Egypt for four hundred years.

Genesis 15: 13 – "And he said unto Abram, know of a surety that thy seed shall be a stranger in a land that is not theirs, *and shall serve then; and they shall afflict them four <u>hundred</u> years;* *

(sta) 120. – By mathematical implication, trumpets are associated with Abram, and with God's foretelling of the Hebrew people's destiny.

Genesis 50: 26 – "So Joseph died, being an <u>hundred</u> and ten years old: and they embalmed him, and he was put in a coffin in Egypt."

(sta) 121. - By biblical implication, trumpets are associated with Joseph, with his years spent in Egypt, and with his death there.

It is a matter of interest that: As was Jacob, his father, Joseph was embalmed, but unlike his father, Joseph's bones were not removed to Canaan and buried in the Promised Land, at least not right away. But the good news, (as is recorded in the book of Exodus, Chapter13, verse19), is that, two hundred years afterword, when Moses led his people out of Egyptian bondage, he took the bones of Joseph with him, and Joseph was eventually buried in the land of Canaan.

Now we will treat with the number 4, the second component of 104:

Again, as with the component number 100, the trumpet associations derived from the number 4 are arrived at as a matter of mathematical implication, not by direct linkage established in biblical verses, and again as with the number 100, trumpet associations derived from the number 4 are nevertheless informative and significant.

The number 4 is the second component of 104. The number 104 is the total number of times that our four trumpet words, trump, trumpet, trumpeter, and trumpets are mentioned in the bible.

(Four)

Genesis 1: 14-19 – *"And God said, Let their be lights in the firmament of the heaven to divide the day from the night: and let them be for signs, and for seasons, and for days, and years.*

And let them be for lights in the firmament of the heaven to give light upon the earth: and it was so.

And God made two great lights; the greater light to rule the day, and the lesser light to rule the night: he made the stars also.

And God set them in the firmament of the heaven to give life upon the earth.

And to rule over the day and over the night, and to divide the light from the darkness: and God saw that it was good.

And the evening and the day were the <u>fourth</u> day."

(sta) 122. - By mathematical implication, trumpets are associated with the creation narrative wherein God chose the fourth day to complete the creation of the physical world, and the universe of which it is a part.

Genesis 2: 10-14 - *"And a river went out of Eden to water the garden, and from thence it was parted, and became unto <u>four</u> heads.*

235

The name of the first is Pison; that is it which compasseth the whole land of Havilah, where there is gold.

And the gold of that land is good: there is bdellium and the onyx stone.

And the name of the second river is Gihon: the same is it that compasseth the whole land of Ethiopia.

And the name of the third river is Hiddekel: that is it which goeth toward the east of Assyria. And the <u>fourth</u> river is Euphrates."

(sta) 123. - By mathematical implication, trumpets are associated with the creation narrative, wherein the four rivers that encompass it describe the location of the Garden of Eden.

Genesis 33: 1 – "And Jacob lifted up his eyes, and looked, and beheld, Esau came, and with him four hundred men. And he divided the children unto Leah, and unto Rachel, and unto the two handmaids."

(sta) 124. – By mathematical implication, trumpets are associated with Jacob and Esau, and with the fact of their loving reunion.

By combining the scriptural significance (established by mathematical implication) associated with these two numbers, 100, and four, which are components of 104, (the total number of times our theme words, trump, trumpet, trumpeter, and trumpets are mentioned in the Bible) we find additional trumpet associations, leading us to conclude that over-all, trumpets play an important role in indicating and emphasizing some of the Bibles important themes, truths, lessons, and commandments.

And so ends Chapter Thirty-three

Chapter Thirty-three yields fifteen significant trumpet associations:

(sta) 111. - By mathematical implication, trumpets are associated with age, longevity, and fertility.

(sta) – 112 - By mathematical implication, trumpets are associated with a walk with God In this life, followed by an eternal walk with God in the next.

(sta) 113. - By mathematical implication trumpets are associated with hope for the future and trust in the Lord.

(sta) 114. – By mathematical implication trumpets are associated with God's displeasure with indiscriminate satisfaction of carnal desires by mankind.

(sta) 115. – By mathematical implication trumpets are associated with impending judgment by God.

(sta) 116. – By mathematical implication trumpets are associated with the reduction of mankind's longevity, and/or with God's warning of his intention to destroy some, or all of what He has created.

(sta) 117. – By mathematical implication trumpets are associated with the process of measuring things, particularly with the process of building the ark.

(sta) 118. – By mathematical implication trumpets are associated with the hope of mankind for salvation, for the rapture of the church, and for eternal reward as companions of God in His kingdom to come.

(sta) 119. - By mathematical implication, trumpets are associated with counting the numbers of things; in particular with how many days the waters of Noah's flood remained fully on the earth, and how many days it took for the waters to completely drain off.

(sta) 120. – By mathematical implication, trumpets are associated with Abram, and with God's foretelling of the Hebrew people's destiny.

(sta) 121. - By mathematical implication, trumpets are associated with Joseph, with his years spent in Egypt, and with his death there.

(sta) 122. - By mathematical implication, trumpets are associated with the creation narrative wherein God chose the fourth day to complete the creation of the physical world, and the universe of which it is a part.

(sta) 123. - By mathematical implication, trumpets are associated with the creation narrative, wherein the four rivers that encompass it describe the location of the Garden of Eden.

(sta) 124. – By mathematical implication, trumpets are associated with Jacob and Esau, and with the fact of their loving reunion.

Notes and Reflections

Chapter Thirty-Four

Significant trumpet associations derived from a brief study of numbers as they relate to trumpets as derived from the New Testament

The New Testament:

The New Testament of the bible is made up of 27 Books.

Of these 27 books, five contain verses wherein one or more of the four words (trump, trumpet, trumpeter, and trumpets) that identify the subject matter of this current work, "Softly The Trumpet" are mentioned.

In these 5 books the four words combined are mentioned 14 times. The number 14 is biblically significant. Therefore fourteen becomes our number of interest.

Because the number 14 is biblically significant, we do not parse its component numbers.

Whenever a trumpet association is prompted by scriptural mention of the number 14, the resulting significant trumpet association is understood to be established by mathematical implication.

The New Testament fulfills, completes, and satisfies the themes, truths, lessons, and commandments established in the Old Testament. Therefore each mention of the number fourteen (our number of interest) recorded in the New Testament is considered to be indicative of a significant trumpet association, and may refer to a verse in either the Old or New Testament.

The New Testament mentions the number 14, five times: Matthew 1: 17,

Acts 27: 27, Acts 27: 33, 2 Corinthians 12: 2, and Galatians 2: 1:

Matthew 1: 17 – "So all the generations from Abraham to David are fourteen generations; and from David until the carrying away into Babylon are fourteen generations; and from the carrying away into Babylon unto Christ are fourteen generations."

Matthew 1: 17 ^ incorporates three persons of particular importance: Abraham, David, and Jesus. Relevant verses and brief commentary regarding Abraham and David follow below:

Abraham played an extremely important role in God's plan for mankind, particularly regarding God's covenant promises to him:

Genesis 17: 6-9

"And I will make thee exceeding fruitful, and I will make nations of thee, and kings shall come out of thee.

And I will establish my covenant between me and thee and thy seed after thee in their generations for an everlasting covenant, to be a God unto thee, and to thy seed after thee.

And I will give unto thee, and to thy seed after thee, the land wherein thou art a stranger, and all the land of Canaan, for an everlasting possession; and I will be their God.

And God said unto Abraham Thou shalt keep my covenant therefore, thou, and thy seed after thee in their generations."

David is the next biblical personage mentioned in Matthew's lead-up to the arrival of Jesus on the scene of history.

David was the king of all Israel, the second king of the Untied KIngdom. Among the many mentions of David recorded in the Bible are the following:

He slew the Philistine giant Goliath with his slingshot loaded with a stone from a nearby stream.

He attacked and captured the fortified city of Jebus, the city that later became known as Jerusalem.

David' son, Solomon later built the temple at Jerusalem.

David was an accomplished harpist, using his skills to soothe the troubled mind of King Saul, the first king of the United Kingdom.

David moved the Ark of the Covenant to Jerusalem.

In addition to being an accomplished harpist, David was also a gifted Psalmist.

But most important of all, David the great King was the ancestor of Jesus the Christ.

The number 14, featured so prominently in Matthew 1: 17, is arrived at by use of a technique called "gematria", whereby a numerical value is assigned to the consonants of a word and none to its vowels.

Using number values assigned to letters in the Hebrew alphabet, David's name adds up to 14 - (D=4, V=6, D=4) = 14.

It is because of David's overall importance in the history of the Old Testament, but especially because David was Jesus' ancestor, that the gospel of Matthew uses the numerical value of David's name to structure the genealogy of Jesus into three groups of fourteen generations. The groups include: the generations from Abraham to David, the generations from David until the carrying away into Babylon, and the generations from the carrying away into Babylon unto Jesus the Christ.

Jesus is a bona fide descendant of David, and therefor is considered to be a 'Son of David' in accordance with the Hebrew definition and usage of the term.

Not only is Jesus the rightful heir to the throne of David in accordance with Israel's rules of kingly ascension, but also, and more importantly, Jesus is God, the King of all creation.

(sta) 125. — By mathematical implication, trumpets are associated with a reminder of Abraham's important role as

recorded in the Old Testament, particularly regarding God's covenant promises to him.

(sta) 126. – By mathematical implication trumpets are associated with the great king David, warrior, worshiper, psalmist, and ancestor of Jesus the Christ.

(sta) 127. – By mathematical implication, trumpets are associated with our Lord and Savior, Jesus the Christ; that He came into this world, born king of the Jews, and King of all Kings.

David is the key to the throne of Israel and to the throne of heaven because God promised David a kingdom that would have no end. – 2 Samuel 7: 13, 16:

2 Samuel 7: 13 – "He shall build an house for my name, and I will stablish the throne of his kingdom forever."

2 Samuel 7: 16 – "And thine house and thy kingdom shall be established for ever before thee: thy throne shall be established for ever."

Interestingly, Jesus' right to the throne of David is well documented, and yet, His lawful kingships of the secular and spiritual kingdoms continues to be denied by the people He came to save, the nation of Israel. Of all people, the elite of Jewry should know better. When Jesus arrived on the scene, He assumed the mantle of spiritual king of Israel, but He did not press the issue of His legitimate earthly kingship. Remember what He told Pilate: - *"My kingdom is not of this world: if my kingdom were of this world, then would my servants fight, that I should not be delivered to the Jews: but now is my kingdom not from hence." – John 18: 36*

The next book of the New Testament that mentions 14 (our number of interest) is the book of Acts:

King Agrippa determines to send Paul to Italy to be judged by the highest Roman authority, Caesar. On the journey a terrible storm arises, and the crew decides to abandon ship, but Paul persuades them not to, explaining that an angel of God had assured him that he and the crew would arrive safely at their destination if they remained on the ship. As a result of Paul's importuning, the crew survives the storm.

Acts 27: 27 – "But when the fourteenth night was come, as were driven up and down in Adria, about midnight the shipmen deemed that they drew near to some country."

Acts 27: 33 – "And while the day was coming on, Paul besought them all to take meat, saying, This day is the fourteenth day that ye have tarried and continued fasting, having taken nothing."

Acts 27: 34 – "Wherefore I pray you to take some meat: for this is for your health: for there shall not an hair fall from the head of any of you."

The number fourteen is associated with Salvation.

Because of Paul's spiritual strength, his absolute trust in God, he and the crew were delivered from an almost certain physical death.

(sta) 128. – By mathematical implication, trumpets are associated with Paul and the good news he brought of salvation thru Jesus the Christ.

Not only did Paul urge his shipmates to eat the meat necessary for their physical well being, but by preaching the truth of Jesus the Messiah, he fed them the spiritual "meat" they needed to endure life's sometimes frightening vicissitudes.

Do you yearn for some of that spiritual meat? You can have some right now! The words of Paul, his spiritual certitude and his love of God are just as fresh today as they were then. Yes the values of this world are necessary to survive in this world, but the peace of mind, the strength to keep going when the going gets tough; they come from spiritual values, from the love of Jesus, from the faith that is ours for the taking. The Holy Spirit of God is ready to fill the void within you with confidence in the future, with the strength of spiritual conviction.

These words I write are not just empty platitudes; they are the essence of what the greatest book ever written tells us time and time again: You are not alone; God is with you; God sent His Son to show His love for you. Give God a chance. If you are lost, and you want to take the first step in finding God, listen to what Jesus says as he rebuffs the Pharisees who ask Jesus a contentious question:

Matthew 22: 34-40

"But when the Pharisees had heard that he had put the Sadducees to silence, they were gathered together.

Then one of them which was a lawyer, asked him a question, tempting him, and saying,

Master, which is the great commandment in the law?

Jesus said unto him,

Thou shalt love thy God with all thy heart, and with all thy soul, and with all thy mind.

This is the first and great commandment.

And the second is like unto it, Thou shalt love thy neighbor as thyself.

On these two commandments hang all the law and the prophets."

Think about that for a minute! – Inspired by the Holy Spirit of God, numerous writers, over a period of thousands of years compose, and/or write a book comprised of sixty-six books. This great book –The Holy Bible - contains the wisdom of the ages expressed in many thousands of words. And yet, Jesus is able to synthesize the Bible's purpose and wisdom down to a few verses and a few words. No wonder the so-called religious experts, the Sadducees and the Pharisees, were flummoxed. They had no answer to Jesus; they never had the answer to Jesus. He was a problem.

Their solution to the Jesus problem was to have Him killed. They managed to do that by maneuvering the Roman authorities into crucifying him unto death. But they found out that Jesus is like the truth; the truth does not stay dead and neither did Jesus. Within three days of his death and entombment, Jesus rose from the dead in truth and in glory, and put the lie to the religious elite who rejected their Messiah. Rather than accepting Him, they chose to maintain their status quo as lovers and seekers of power, lust, greed, and pride.

The next book of the New Testament that mentions 14 (our number of interest) is the book of 2 Corinthians:

2 Corinthians 12: 1-6

12: 1 – "It is not expedient for me doubtless to glory. I will come to visions and revelations of the Lord."

12: 2 – "I knew a man in Christ above fourteen years ago, (whether in the body, I cannot tell; or whether out of the body, I cannot tell: God knoweth;) such an one caught up to the third heaven."

12" 3 _ "And I knew such a man, (whether in the body or out of the body, I cannot tell: God knoweth;")

12: 4 – "How that he was caught up into paradise, and heard unspeakable words, which it is not lawful for a man to utter."

12: 5 – "Of such an one will I glory: yet of myself I will not glory, but in mine infirmities."

12: 6 – For though I would desire to glory, I shall not be a fool; for I will say the truth: but now I forbear, lest any man should think of me above that which he seeth me to be, or that he heareth of me." ∗

* - In these verses, his second letter to the Corinthians, Paul recalls that fourteen years prior, he was "caught up", either physically, or in vision, to the third heaven where God dwells. Paul acknowledges that, (being human, and therefore subject to ordinary glory-lust) it would be tempting to reveal what he saw and heard whilst in heaven, but he forbears doing so, so that the Corinthians would think of him and judge him in more normal terms, rather than as one who reveals sights seen, and words heard in God's dwelling place.

Had Paul revealed the full extent of God's blessings on him, it would have been extremely difficult for the Corinthians to think of him as an ordinary man.

(sta)129. – By mathematical implication, trumpets are associated with the humility of Paul and on his unrelenting focus on the person of Jesus the risen Christ.

(sta)130. – By mathematical implication, trumpets are associated with Paul's ministry, and with the fact that spiritual blessings were bestowed on him.

The next book of the New Testament that mentions 14 (our number of interest) is the book of Galatians:

Galatians 2: 1 – "Then fourteen years after I went up again to Jerusalem with Barnabas, and took Titus with me also.

The earliest converts to Christianity were Jews, and as a matter of tradition and convenience many of them continued to attend services and worship in the synagogues.

Many of them - (the Judaizers) - were of the opinion that Gentiles converting to Christianity must first be in full compliance with God's Covenant stipulations given to Abraham regarding circumcision:

<u>Genesis 17: 9-10</u>

"And God said unto Abraham, Thou shalt keep my covenant therefore, thou and thy seed after thee in their generations.

This is my covenant, which ye shall keep, between me and you and thy seed after thee; Every man child among you shall be circumcised."

But Paul believed and preached that the new church, instituted by Jesus prior to His death and resurrection and fully empowered by the Holy Spirit on Pentecost, proclaims that salvation is come by the grace of God, not by adherence to Mosaic Law.

Fourteen years after visiting Peter and James at Jerusalem, Paul returns to Jerusalem accompanied by Titus and Barnabas. At Jerusalem, Paul confers with the Apostles regarding the legitimacy of his preaching to Gentile believers; that circumcision is not required of them in order to join the Church of Jesus Christ.

It is these discussions and others stemming from them, that certain nascent ideas, such as, we are not saved by good works or by strict obedience to Mosaic Law, - take deeper root, eventually flowering into widely held doctrine.

(sta) 131. – By mathematical implication, trumpets are associated with Paul's absolute belief in the truths made known to him, including that the doctrine of uncircumcision is an expression of God's will.

And so ends Chapter Thirty-four.

Chapter Thirty-four yields seven significant trumpet associations:

(sta) 125. – By mathematical implication, trumpets are associated with a reminder of Abraham's important role as recorded in the Old Testament, particularly regarding God's covenant promises to him.

(sta) 126. – By mathematical implication trumpets are associated with the great king David, warrior, worshiper, psalmist, and ancestor of Jesus the Christ.

(sta) 127. – By mathematical implication, trumpets are associated with our Lord and Savior, Jesus Christ; that He came into this world, born king of the Jews, and King of all kings.

(sta) 128. – By mathematical implication, trumpets are associated with Paul and the good news he brought of salvation thru Jesus Christ.

(sta)129. – By mathematical implication, trumpets are associated with the humility of Paul and on his unrelenting focus on the person of Jesus the risen Christ.

(sta)130. – By mathematical implication, trumpets are associated with Paul's ministry, and with the fact that spiritual blessings were bestowed on him.

(sta) 131. – By mathematical implication, trumpets are associated with Paul's absolute belief in the truths made known to him, including that the doctrine of uncircumcision is an expression of God's will.

Notes and Reflections

Chapter Thirty-Five

Significant trumpet associations derived from a brief study of numbers as they relate to Old Testament mentions of our New Testament number of interest, (14) as found in the book of Genesis.

The Old Testament book of Genesis, (the theme setter for the entire Bible), mentions 14, our New Testament number of interest, three times: Genesis 14: 5, Genesis 31: 41, and Genesis 46: 22:

Genesis 14: 5 – "And in the fourteenth year came Chedorlaomer, and the kings that were with him, and smote the Rephaims in Ashteroth Karnaim, and the Zuzims in Ham, and the Emins in Shaveh Kiriatham,"

Thus we are presented with the first war recorded in sacred Scripture. Because it is recorded in Genesis, the first book of the Bible, we can be sure that wars are an integral part of the history and habits of mankind.

This war took place in a place called, the vale of Siddim, a name which translates into modern English as, "the valley of the dead sea". What an apt description that is! The sea is dead because of high mineral content (mostly salt), and the valley on which the war was conducted, is associated with death because of those who died there.

(sta) 132. – By mathematical implication, trumpets are associated with war.

The relationship of trumpets with war constitutes the strongest trumpet association with any biblical theme, truth, lesson, or commandment. The following, previously recorded significant trumpet associations related to war, testify to that fact:

(sta) 16. - When Israel goes to war in their own land against their oppressors, if the trumpets are blown by Aaron's priests, and in a manner obedient to God' specific instruction, God will look on Israel with favor and will save Israel..

(sta) 18. – The sounds of the trumpets served the people of Israel as signals to assemble, march, commence war and celebrate sacred feast days of holy convocations.

(sta) 19. – The beginning of the fall of Jericho starts when Israel complies with God's puzzling command to initiate a battle campaign featuring the blare of trumpets as the chief weaponry.

(sta) 41. – In ancient times, the trumpet is like a firearm, in that, when under the control of good men, it can be used for good purposes – (self defense, protection of the innocent, the conduct of just wars, etc.), whereas when under the control of treacherous men, the trumpet can be used to carry out nefarious schemes of deception such as envisioned by Absalom, and for other evil purposes.

(sta) 42. - *The trumpet blare can begin a war, or sound the peace.*

(sta) 59. – *The final trumpet of the war between Abijah and Jeroboam, between Judah and Israel, sounded the death knell of a nation gone wrong- Israel), and the ascendancy of a nation-(Judah) obedient to God's will.*

(sta) 70. – *God extolls the virtues of one of his created creatures, the warhorse, pointing out that this fearsome animal disregards the danger signaled by the blaring trumpets.*

(sta) 71. –*As the trumpets blare comes closer and closer, and their fearsome scream grows louder and louder, the warhorse understands what they mean, but true to its created nature it paws the ground in destiny fulfilling anticipation.*

(sta) 75. – *When an army's ensign is displayed and its trumpets blare, or otherwise aggressively bellow justification for warfare, sooner or later war is coming; sooner more likely than later.*

(sta) 79. - *Sometimes the trumpet sound is thought to be synonymous with the alarm of war, or even, given its unmistakable association with battles, with the sound and fury of pitched battles, the clash of weapons, the frightening sounds of wounded men crying, and the last gasps of soldiers dying.*

(sta) 80 - *Wars and rumors of wars can arrive in the blink of an eye, but once the war arrives, the enemy insignia can remain on display and the war trumpets can blare, for what seem like a lifetime. For those who die, it is a lifetime.*

(sta) 81. - The threat to Judah of invasions was a constant, and so too was the necessity of having trumpets and bonfires available at a moment's notice for the purposes of warning, mobilization and preparation for war.

(sta) 83. - The sounds of the trumpets of war had become synonymous with - (virtually, as terrible and fear inducing as the actuality of it) - the sounds and sights of war: the dead and the dying, the suffering of the wounded; their cries of pain and hopelessness, the silent despair, knowing that to survive intact meant to fight another day, or even synonymous with the hope of receiving a serious wound, but not too serious.

(sta) 84. - The spectacle of a standard flapping in the wind accompanied by the blare of a war trumpet had the potential of inspiring soldiers to perform deeds of great valor in battle. Such potential was sometimes realized, but not always.

(sta) 86. - If, as has happened many times, the people of Israel choose to ignore God's commands (in this case His warning trumpet) and a weapon of war (either a physical sword or a spiritual lapse) injures physical or spiritual lives, then it will be their own fault. Figuratively and literally, their own blood will be on their own hands.

(sta) 87 - He who heeds the word of God, the warning of God, the trumpet of God; he will be saved physically and spiritually.

(sta) 89. - Alas, Israel, as stiff-necked and stubborn as ever, refuses to even hear the word of God delivered by the trumpet's blare, never-mind, to actually heed it.

(sta) 91. – During a time of great strife in Judah, Joel the prophet called for the trumpet to blare a warning of forthcoming invasions.

The next mention of 14, our New Testament number of interest, as found in the Old Testament book of Genesis is Genesis 31: 41:

Genesis 31: 41 – "Thus have I been twenty years in thy house; I served thee fourteen years for thy daughters, and six years for thy cattle: and thou hast changed my wages ten times." *

* - As per the Lord's intention that Jacob separates himself and his family from the spiritually unfavorable domination of his uncle Laban. Jacob spews out his anger and resentment:

(sta) 133. - By mathematical implication, trumpets are associated with counting and emphasis.

The next mention of 14, our New Testament number of interest, as found in the Old Testament book of Genesis is Genesis 46: 22:

Genesis 46: 22 – "These are the sons of Rachel, which were born to Jacob: all the souls were fourteen.

(sta.) 134. – By mathematical implication, trumpets are associated with counting and keeping track of the genealogy of important biblical personages such as Jacob, whose genealogical thread culminates in Jesus.

And so ends Chapter Thirty-five

Chapter thirty-five yields three significant trumpet associations:

(sta) 132. – By mathematical implication, trumpets are associated with war.

(sta) 133. – By mathematical implication, trumpets are associated with counting and emphasis.

(sta) 134. - – By mathematical implication, trumpets are associated with counting and keeping track of the genealogy of important biblical personages such as Jacob, whose genealogical thread culminates in Jesus.

Our next chapter (36) presents an overview of significant trumpet associations thus far gleaned from sacred Scripture. The first grouping, (sta) 1 through 110 is comprised of those derived from direct scriptural mention.

The second grouping, (sta) 111 through 134 is arrived at by means of 'mathematical implication.'

Notes and Reflections

Chapter Thirty-Six

For reasons of clarity, emphasis, quick reference and overview, all of the significant trumpet associations thus far gleaned from our reading of Sacred Scripture are sequentially listed below:

Group 1

(sta) 1. – - The sound of the trumpet can serve as a herald of an appearance or action by the Lord.

(sta) 2. – The sound of trumpets exceedingly loud engenders fear and respect for the power of the Lord.

(sta) 3. – The long and very loud trump of the trumpet foretells, and announces the presence and/or spoken word of the Lord God of heaven.

(sta) 4. – Trumpets are associated with the voice of God.

(sta) 5. – Trumpets are associated with the prohibition against idol worship.

(sta) 6. – Trumpets are associated with God's desired behavior of men and women towards other men and women.

(sta) 7. – Trumpets are associated with God's desired behavior of men and women towards God, particularly regarding obedience and worship.

(sta) 8. - God established the Feast of Trumpets as a special memorial feast day emphasizing its innate and as yet, not fully realized (in terms of recognition and appreciation) importance in sacred Scripture.

(sta) 9. – The Feast of Trumpets is the linchpin of God's sacred feast days, days of holy convocations, days of sacred gatherings.

(sta) 10. - The trumpet sound is closely associated with the Fiftieth Year Jubilee.

(sta) 11. - At God's command two special trumpets of silver were to be made for two special purposes: Calling the camp to assemble in front of the Tabernacle, and informing the camp when it was time to move.

(sta) 12. - The trumpet sounding from just one of these special trumpets informed that only the camp leaders were to assemble, and it was their responsibility to pass along to their charges specific, and/or additional information.

(sta)13. - As recorded in the book of Numbers, verses 5 & 6 ^, the trumpet sound was used to signal when to march, and in what direction, but also the specific order of march.

(sta) 14. - In the wilderness, God established Aaron as the high priest, and in perpetuity, the sons of Aaron would be forever the source from which the priesthood is drawn, commanding

and controlling Israel by the blowing of the trumpets in the manner and on the occasions commanded by God.

(sta) 15. - *Throughout the generations of Israel, (those living under the Law of Moses) are as fully obligated to obey the trumpet's commands, blown by the priests of Aaron, as they are the laws of Moses given by God.*

(sta) 16. - *When Israel goes to war in their own land against their oppressors, if the trumpets are blown by Aaron's priests, and in a manner obedient to God' specific instruction, God will look on Israel with favor and will save them.*

(sta)17. - *The trumpets served the Jews as their memorial to God, a reminder to them that He is their Lord and their God.*

(sta) 18. – *The sounds of the trumpets served the people of Israel as signals to assemble, march, commence war and celebrate sacred feast days of holy convocations.*

(sta) 19. – *The beginning of the fall of Jericho starts when Israel complies with God's puzzling command to initiate a battle campaign featuring the blare of trumpets as the chief weaponry.*

(sta) 20. - *In order for God's perfect plan for the taking of Jericho to succeed, the people of Israel were required to follow the plan exactly, including the blaring of the trumpets, and the great shouts of the people.*

(sta) 21. - *Combined with complete and specific obedience to God's commands, the great blare of the trumpets magnified by the deafening screams of the people brought down the walls of Jericho.*

But more importantly, because it was God's will that they fall, the walls of Jericho did fall. The people and the troops, the priests and Joshua, and the trumpets served God's purpose, teaching two valuable lessons: With God all things are possible, but without God all roads lead to disaster.

(sta) 22. - Throughout the long tragic years that have passed since the walls of Jericho succumbed to the power of God's trumpets, had Israel continued in unswerving obedience to His will, the history of Israel would depict a more joyful, inspirational journey. When Jesus came to them in love and forgiveness two thousand years ago, instead of rejecting their Messiah, they would have embraced him. Instead of slapping him and spitting on him, they would have opened their hearts and minds to the Holy Spirit, and instead of arranging for his death on the cross, they would have worshiped and glorified Jesus as the rightful heir to the throne of David and the Messiah they had long waited for.

But that is not the road they traveled, those are not the decisions they made. And as a result, when Jesus comes again, only a remnant of Israel will be there to finally say, "My Lord and my God."

(sta) 23. - Although it is not stated specifically and is a conclusion arrived at by extrapolation of peripheral information, trumpets significantly emphasize that in order for Israel to survive as a nation, it must obey God.

(sta) 24. – Trumpets are a reminder that God is complete and perfect. As a collateral benefit of God's completeness and perfection, we can conclude that his plan for our salvation is also complete and perfect.

(sta) 25. – *Trumpets played a significant role in the battle of Jericho, a battle of both military and spiritual importance.*

(sta) 26. – *Trumpets played a significant role in the battle of Moab, a battle of both military and spiritual importance.*

(sta) 27. – *Preparing to battle Israel's oppressors the Midianites, Gideon blows a trumpet, calling his clan the Abiezerites, to join the ranks of his army.*

(sta) 28. – *In accordance with God's seemingly peculiar battle plan, Gideon prepares his meager, three hundred-strong-army by arming them with only trumpets, jars, and torches*

(sta) 29. – *To those willing to acknowledge the collateral, spiritual significance of the instruments chosen by God to facilitate the carrying out of his will, the sound of the trumpet, whether heard physically or perceived spiritually can serve to remind us of certain truths.*

(sta) 30. - *God expects full compliance with his commands regardless of any perceived inconsistency with human logic regarding their content or with his means of communicating them, whether by trumpets, or other chosen instruments.*

(sta) 31. – *God's choice of weapons for Israel against Midian (trumpets, jars, torches) teaches us that it is folly to pick and choose, to decide that some of God's commands are in error or illogical, or without merit and to conclude therefore that it is safe to ignore or disobey them.*

(sta) 32. - As proven in the battle of Midian, fear can be a more decisive factor than many thousands of conventional weapons

(sta) 33. - Our battle on earth is choosing between good and evil, between physical and spiritual. God's battle is with the devil.

God will win his battle. But how about you and me, will we heed the messages of the trumpets and His other chosen instruments?

Let's cash in with the winning ticket: Be good; embrace spiritual values.

(sta) 34. - Trumpets played a significant role in the battle of Midian, a battle of both military and spiritual importance.

(sta) 35. – – Trumpet sounds were customized to convey their intended messages by varying the pitch and duration of fluctuating multiples of trumpets relayed from one outpost to the next. This tactic was instrumental in allowing Israel to achieve military victories beyond her numerical strength.

(sta) 36. – Midst the hills of Ammah, in the wilderness of Gibeon the trumpet sounds the end of a battle whilst there still remains a remnant of the foe available for pursuit and slaughter, a significant departure from the traditional aftermath of such an encounter. In this instance however the trumpet was significantly associated with the cause of peace and mercy.

(sta) 37 - The trumpet sound is the sound of heaven's will, whether they are blared in good times or bad, and whether or

not they are instrumental in various stages of armed conflict, or (when at God's command more than three thousand years ago) they announced and celebrated that most important holyday The Feast of Trumpets, a day decreed by God to be a day of "holy convocation", a day of rest and a day wherein the blowing of trumpets is done as a memorial.

(sta) 38. – Sometimes, depending on who is observing and doing the listening, the trumpet sound can say, "Look at me, look at me, look at what I have done. I am dancing and leaping with joy because I am great" or it can say," Look, look at what God hath wrought. I am leaping and dancing with joy because our Lord our God is great."

(sta) 39. - The sound of trumpets can sometimes signal great joy and spiritual fervor. Those who are one with the Lord in obedience and love may rightfully join the party. Those who are not truly onboard, neither in faith nor in love and find ways to attack the righteously elated, often disguising their hate filled motives under the guise of moral indignation,

(sta) 40. – When the trumpet sound signals a time of great joy and spiritual fervor, those who attack the righteously elated do so at great peril to their physical and spiritual health.

(sta) 41. – In ancient times, the trumpet is like a firearm, in that, when under the control of good men, it can be used for good purposes – (self defense, protection of the innocent, the conduct of just wars, etc.), whereas when under the control of treacherous men, the trumpet can be used to carry out nefarious schemes of deception such as envisioned by Absalom and for other evil purposes.

(sta) 42. - The trumpet blare can begin a war, or sound the peace.

(sta) 43. - An initial trumpet sound can be the rallying signal that promises the fresh start of a new day, the imminent crowning of a more righteous king, or the establishment of a fairer government more sympathetic to the needs of the people.

(sta) 44. — Whatever the aspirations of the author of the initial trumpet sound and regardless of the methods employed to attain the goals promised, if the aspirations or the methods are in conflict with God's intentions, the final blare of the trumpet will serve as a death knell, (whether physical, and/or spiritual) of the initial promisor, and of his promises.

(sta) 45. — When next Jesus comes again, the trumpet sound will signal the initiation of the transformation from corruptible physical bodies to incorruptible spiritual ones, both for the living, and for the dead in Christ.

(sta) 46. - No trumpet sound accompanied Adonijah's failed attempt to become king. Unless it is within the realm of God's will, no trumpet lends credence to a coronation.

(sta) 47 - — The trumpet's blare may pronounce the accomplishment of God's will, and/or celebrate the inspired recognition of His will be done.

(sta) 48 - When the trumpet serves God's purpose, its sound is heavenly, whether celebratory or congratulatory, or when solemn-sad or happily glad and all the steps between. Then it is heaven sent, God's chosen instrument.

(sta) 49. – *The trumpet's blare may pronounce the accomplishment of God's will, and/or celebrate the inspired recognition of His will be done.*

(sta) 50. - *Depending on which side of life's equation one inhabits, either the carnal -(lover and seeker of worldly values), or the spiritual –(lover and seeker of spiritual values), the mere presence of lawfully authorized trumpeters can strike fear, or engender joy.*

(sta) 51. - *Divinely authorized trumpeters sounding God's chosen instruments can designate specifically targeted recipients as Schemers, Dreamers, or Believers.*

(sta) 52. – *In order to comply fully with God's intentions regarding temple worship and rituals, it is necessary that certain sacred objects, including trumpets be on hand and at the ready.*

(sta) 53. – *Joyful sounding trumpets may blare, but even if initiated at the behest of the greatest of earthly kings, without God's sanction they portend sad consequences.*

(sta) 54. – *Joyful trumpets may blare and even if sounded at the behest of the least of us, with God's sanction they portend good news.*

(sta) 55. – *Celebrating the installation of the Ark of God at Jerusalem, Israel experienced one of her finest moments:*

She adhered to tradition, i.e., properly clad singers, duly authorized via custom and heritage), with their sons and brethren furnished with cymbals, psalteries, and harps, led by 120 priests playing the trumpets, united, one and all, worshiping the one true God, the God of Abraham, Isaac, and Jacob.

(sta) 56. – Celebrating the installation of the Ark of God at Jerusalem, the trumpeters and singers blended their sounds in a manner so as to create one voice, possibly constituting the first one-sound combination of trumpet/voice in praise and glory of God.

(sta) 57. - Figuratively, and for all practical purposes, literally, when the trumpets sounded at the dedication ceremony opening the temple at Jerusalem, an entire nation, Israel, God's chosen people, stood, and united in spirit, acknowledged and worshiped the one true God.

(sta) 58. - When the army of Israel demonstrated intention to attack Judah, Abijah caused the trumpets of Judah to sound, virtually as warning from God to cease and desist their futile attempts at dictating which persons and procedures were acceptable in the eyes of God to properly worship Him.

(sta) 59. – The final trumpet of the war between Abijah and Jeroboam, between Judah and Israel, sounded the death knell of a nation gone wrong- Israel), and the ascendancy of a nation-(Judah) obedient to God's will.

(sta) 60. - When the destruction of Judah by Israel seemed imminent and unstoppable, the trumpets sounded and God listened.

(sta) 61. – Psalteries –(small harps, and larger harps, all utilized for their soothing sounds) and the trumpets, which, depending on how played could be soothing to the nerves, or shrill, and sometimes blared with ear shattering volume, were

brought into the temple at Jerusalem to mark and celebrate Judah's great victory over Moab, Ammon and others.

(sta) 62. - Jehoiada choreographed the final scene of Athaliah's downfall and Joash's ascension so that when Athaliah entered the temple to ascertain what all the fuss was about, there stood the newly minted king Joash, celebrated by singers and musical instruments, his kingship undeniably affirmed by the trumpets great blare.

(sta) 63. – At the second sounding of the trumpets Athaliah tore her clothes and cried treason. And that was her final earthly defiance of God's will. Instead of accepting the inevitable execution of 'His Will Be Done', she did not repent, she did not ask for God's forgiveness, nor did she proclaim or exhibit determination to sin no more.

(sta) 64. – The priest's helpers (the Levites) stood with the cymbals, psalteries, and with harps, and the priests stood with the trumpets at the occasion of the restoration of temple worship by king Hezekiah.

(sta) 65. - And when the burnt offerings began at the occasion of the restoration of temple worship by king Hezekiah, the song of the Lord began, and so too did the trumpets, along with the other instruments of invocation, gratitude and worship.

(sta) 66. – Whilst the tremendous numbers of burnt offerings were burning, the congregation worshiped and the trumpets sounded. At the occasion of the restoration of worship at the temple brought about by king Hezekiah, the singers had ample time to sing The Song of the Lord. *

(sta) 67. – The trumpets blare served to pronounce the restoration of worship at the temple in Jerusalem.

(sta) 68. - Not only was the trumpet sound a call for help, but during the rebuilding of the walls of Judah, it also served as a reminder of Nehemiah's promise to those working on the wall that God would fight for them. The trumpet sound can serve as a reminder to the faithful that God is with them.

(sta) 69. – At the dedication ceremony celebrating the rebuilding of the walls of Judah, priests and the sons of priests were tasked with the blowing of the trumpets, thereby demonstrating that trumpets were often used in religious ceremonies and other important occasions.

(sta) 70. – God extolls the virtues of one of his created creatures, the warhorse, pointing out that this fearsome animal disregards the danger signaled by the blaring trumpets.

(sta) 71. –As the trumpets blare comes closer and closer, and their fearsome scream grows louder and louder, the warhorse knows what they portend, but true to its created nature it paws the ground in destiny fulfilling anticipation.

(sta) 72. – From this and other sources, it becomes more apparent that the trumpet sound is closely associated with the comings and goings, or more specifically, to the descending and rising of Jesus the Christ, the Son of God.

(sta) 73. – In addition to their other functions, trumpets were used to signal the opening and closing of ritualistic religious ceremonies.

sta) 74. - Particularly when used during sacred songs (psalms), the use of trumpets helped foster the attainment of a personal relationship with God commensurate with the emotional intensity associated with fervent prayer.

(sta) 75. – When an army's ensign is displayed and its trumpets blare, or otherwise aggressively bellows justification for warfare, sooner or later war is coming; sooner more likely than later.

(sta) 76. – The great trumpet, probably a "shophar" - a trumpet fashioned from a ram's horn, will signal the beginning of God's actions, culminating in Israel's repenting of her past rejections of Jesus and in the fulfillment of the Old and New Testament's promises of salvation for God's chosen people."

(sta) 77. – to assure that Isaiah's words gain Israel's attention, God commanded him to shout like the blast of a trumpet. In terms of getting attention and emphasizing the importance of what follows it, the trumpet sound had no equal in the Old Testament.

(sta) 78. - At a time of danger of attack from the North, (the Babylonians) Isaiah calls for the blowing of the trumpets to serve as a call for national self-examination, and as an urgent call to assemble concurrent with the necessity of withdrawing to fortified cities:

(sta) 79. - Sometimes the trumpet sound is thought to be synonymous with the alarm of war, or even, given its unmistakable association with battles, with the sound and fury of pitched battles, the clash of weapons, the frightening sounds of wounded men crying, and the last gasps of soldiers dying.

(sta) 80 - Wars and rumors of wars can arrive in the blink of an eye, but once the war arrives, the enemy insignia can remain on display and the war trumpets can blare, for what seem like a lifetime. For those who die, it is a lifetime.

(sta) 81. - The threat to Judah of invasions was a constant, and so too was the necessity of having trumpets and bonfires available at a moment's notice for the purposes of warning, mobilization and preparation for war.

(sta) 82. - Provisions were well established to afford adequately early warnings to Judah of impending battles via trumpets, but incredibly the people declined to cooperate. They would not hearken; they would not obey the commands of the Lord

(sta) 83. - The sounds of the trumpets of war had become synonymous with - (virtually, as terrible and fear inducing as the actuality of it) - the sounds and sights of war: the dead and the dying, the suffering of the wounded; their cries of pain and hopelessness, the silent despair, knowing that to survive intact meant to fight another day, or even synonymous with the hope receiving a serious wound, but not too serious.

(sta) 84. - The spectacle of a standard flapping in the wind accompanied by the blare of a war trumpet had the potential of inspiring soldiers to perform deeds of great valor in battle. Such potential was sometimes realized, but not always.

(sta) 85. – Trumpets may sound, but they carry out their intended effects only if it is God's will that they do so.

(sta) 86. - If, as has happened many times, the people of Israel choose to ignore God's commands (in this case His warning

trumpet) and a weapon of war (either a physical sword or a spiritual lapse) injures physical or spiritual lives, then it will be their own fault. Figuratively and literally, their own blood will be on their own hands.

(sta) 87 - He who heeds the word of God, the warning of God, the trumpet of God; he will be saved physically and spiritually.

(sta) 88. – If the watchman, cognizant of the imminent threat, fails in his duty to blow the trumpet, the people will be judged and the watchman held accountable for their physical and spiritual sentences.

(sta) 89. - Alas, Israel, as stiff-necked and stubborn as ever, refuses to even hear the word of God delivered by the trumpet's blare, never-mind, to actually heed it.

(sta) 90. - The time is now. The Assyrian enemy (depicted as an eagle) hovers over the house of Israel. Now! Blow the trumpet. Now!

(sta) 91. – During a time of great strife in Judah, Joel the prophet called for the trumpet to blare a warning of forthcoming invasions.

(sta) 92. - And again during a time of great strife in Judah, Joel called for the trumpet to blare, this time as a call to gather in solemn assembly for the purpose of promoting a rededication to the Lord God of Creation, and to possibly illuminate the people regarding Joel's prophecy regarding the reality of the Son of God, the Rapture of his church, and of his his righteous judgment upon the living and the dead.

(sta) 93. – Because of Moab's intransigence, desecrating the body of the king of Edom, exacting personal vengeance, and thereby usurping the authority and power of God, Moab pays with his life.

(sta) 94. - As further evidence of God's displeasure with Edom, not only is the king killed, but so also are all the princes!

This spells the end of Edom, forever.

(sta) 95. – Sometimes not even God's warning trumpet is enough to convince sinners to repent.

(sta) 96. - The day of warning and of war against the fortified cities is at hand. There is no place to hide, no port secure from the oncoming storm. The only safe harbor is that which you decided to pass by - the love and worship of the one true God. Instead you chose the trumpet of war over the love of the Almighty, and you chose the wanton fierceness of God's surrogates over the mercy and forgiveness He repeatedly implored you to accept.

(sta) 97. - Herein is the promise of the Lord, that the Lord will be Israel's champion in battle, that the Lord will blow the trumpet of certain victory over the enemies of the remnant of His chosen people.

(sta) 98. - One of Jesus' pet peeves was hypocrisy, a highly developed characteristic of Israel's religious elite as exemplified by the Pharisees and the temple priests. Often times their religious fervor and ostentatious adoration of God were nothing more than ("Look at me, aren't I wonderful?") attention seeking ploys.

In other words, Jesus tells His disciples, When you pray don't announce yourself with blaring trumpets; instead, reach out to the Lord your creator with unfeigned fervor, deeply grateful for all the gifts He has bestowed on you and on all of mankind

(sta) 99. - If what you seek is the recognition, praise and approval of your fellow man, rather than God's love and gift of eternal salvation, then rest easy:

Simply, blow your own trumpet, - (the louder the better)

Ride the tide of popular opinion.

Be still when your Christian faith is shaken and under attack.

Make sure to abandon the standards of decency, mercy and love you embraced as a child, but which somehow loosed from your grasp as time moved along.

(sta) 100. - The freedom and ability to pray is another precious gift from God. Use it often and well. No trumpet needed.

Within the confines of your inner spirit, seek to bare your soul to the God that made you.

(sta) -101. - If salt loses its saltiness, what is available to flavor the food? If the trumpet loses its proper blare, what is available to sound the alarm?

The Gospels are the Word of God. The trumpet is God's emergency alert. They are both instruments chosen to foster His will.

(sta) – 102. – The "last trump" is the voice of God, His last call to all believers: Come! Join him in eternal peace and happiness. Come! Your reward is great for staying the course. Come! Jesus God, Creator of heaven and earth loves you more than is humanly possible. Come! Bid farewell to the worries of this world. Say hello to your new, incorruptible body. Come! Jesus of Nazareth has prepared a place for you in the kingdom of God.

(sta) 103. – The trumpet sound combined with the terrible punishment commanded by Moses against the idol-worshipers at Mount Sinai in the Old Testament reflect God's deadly judgments inherent in the Old Covenant, as contrasted with the three thousand Jews who came to Christ as recorded in the New Testament book – "The Acts Of The Apostles", chapter two, verse 41. – "Then the that gladly received his word were baptized: and the same day there were added unto them about three thousand souls."

(sta) 104. – Both in the Old and in the New Testaments, God's chief instrument of choice is the trumpet.

(sta) 105. –Whether portrayed in divine visions purposed to communicate reality, or in instances reflecting direct reality, the trumpet's trump is fashioned and utilized by God to inform and facilitate the carrying out of His divine will.

(sta)106. - Seven angels chosen by God will be prepared to sound trumps of coming destructions; the first four of which are intended to convince the as-yet unrepentant to repent before the final three trumpets of destruction sound.

(sta) 107. - An angel of the Lord, flying righteous and true in the very midst of heaven proclaims triple woe to the

remaining inhabitants of the earth. Those who have not met Jesus in the descending clouds of heaven when he raptured his church, or have otherwise failed to repent and accept Jesus of Nazareth as their Lord and Savior will now be subject to the final three, the saddest, most frightening trumpets of God.

(sta) 108. - The four angels bound in the Euphrates, and loosed by the trumpet sound of the sixth angel are demonic, chosen and prepared by God to direct an army of demons as they carry out punishments and destructions on a terrible scale.

(sta) 109. – Pronounced by the seventh angel's trumpet-blare, Jesus, the risen Christ righteously assumes kingship over the kingdoms of the world. Jesus the carpenter, the adopted son of a carpenter, rules the world.

(sta) 110. –As revealed in Revelation 18: 21-22 the absence of pipers and trumpets tolls the silent death knell - (never to rise again), of the ancient city of Babylon, the capital of the evil Babylonian empire wherein idolatry and paganism flourished.

Basically, this book, "Softly Now The Trumpet" attempts to identify significant trumpet associations with the Bible's recorded themes, truths, lessons, and commandments. The results of this effort lead us to focus on two sets of circumstances:

Firstly, those instances, (sta) 1 through 110, shown above, when the verse of Scripture directly mentions one of our four trumpet words –(trump, trumpet, trumpeters, trumpets), and thereby reveal a direct trumpet association with one of more of the Bible's themes, truths, lessons, and commandments;

Secondly, those instances - (sta) 111 through 134, shown as Group 2, below), when the verse of Scripture mentions our 'number of interest', and thereby reveal by mathematical implication, an indirect trumpet association with one or more of the Bible's themes, truths, lessons, and commandments.

Group 2

This method of Biblical investigation – ('Mathematical Implication'), is experimental on this author's part. Hopefully the resulting significant trumpet associations will pique enough scholarly interest to warrant further investigation:

(sta) 111. - By mathematical implication, trumpets are associated with age, longevity, and fertility.

(sta) – 112 - By mathematical implication, trumpets are associated with a walk with God In this life, followed by an eternal walk with God in the next.

(sta) 113. - By mathematical implication trumpets are associated with hope for the future and trust in the Lord.

(sta) 114. – By mathematical implication trumpets are associated with God's displeasure with indiscriminate satisfaction of carnal desires by mankind.

(sta) 115. – By mathematical implication trumpets are associated with impending judgment by God.

(sta) 116. – *By mathematical implication trumpets are associated with the reduction of mankind's longevity, and/or with God's warning of his intention to destroy some, or all of what He has created.*

(sta) 117. – *By mathematical implication trumpets are associated with the process of measuring things, particularly with the process of building the ark.*

(sta) 118. – *By mathematical implication trumpets are associated with the hope of mankind for salvation, for the rapture of the church, and for eternal reward as companions of God in His kingdom to come.*

(sta) 119. - *By mathematical implication, trumpets are associated with counting the numbers of things; in particular with how many days the waters of Noah's flood remained fully on the earth, and how many days it took for the waters to completely drain off.*

(sta) 120. – *By mathematical implication, trumpets are associated with Abram, and with God's foretelling of the Hebrew people's destiny.*

(sta) 121. - *By mathematical implication, trumpets are associated with Joseph, with his years spent in Egypt, and with his death there.*

(sta) 122. - *By mathematical implication, trumpets are associated with the creation narrative wherein God chose the fourth day to complete the creation of the physical world, and the universe of which it is a part.*

(sta) 123. - By mathematical implication, trumpets are associated with the creation narrative, wherein the four rivers that encompass it describe the location of the Garden of Eden.

(sta) 124. – By mathematical implication, trumpets are associated with Jacob and Esau, and with the fact of their loving reunion.

(sta) 125. – By mathematical implication, trumpets are associated with a reminder of Abraham's important role as recorded in the Old Testament, particularly regarding God's covenant promises to him.

(sta) 126. – By mathematical implication, trumpets are associated with the great king David, warrior, worshiper, psalmist, and ancestor of Jesus the Christ.

(sta) 127. - By mathematical implication, trumpets are associated with our Lord and Savior, Jesus Christ; that He came into this world, born king of the Jews, and King of all kings.

(sta) 128. – By mathematical implication, trumpets are associated with Paul and the good news he brought of salvation thru Jesus Christ.

(sta)129. – By mathematical implication, trumpets are associated with the humility of Paul and on his unrelenting focus on the person of Jesus the risen Christ.

(sta)130. – By mathematical implication, trumpets are associated with Paul's ministry, and with the fact that spiritual blessings were bestowed on him.

(sta) 131. – By mathematical implication, trumpets are associated with Paul's absolute belief in the truths made known to him, including that the doctrine of uncircumcision is an expression of God's will.

(sta) 132. – By mathematical implication, trumpets are associated with war.

(sta 133. - By mathematical implication, trumpets are associated with counting and emphasis.

(sta)134. – By mathematical implication, trumpets are associated with counting and keeping track of the genealogy of important biblical personages such as Jacob, whose genealogical thread culminates in Jesus.

And so ends Chapter Thirty-six

Chapter thirty-six yields no new significant trumpet associations.

Notes and Reflections

_____
_____
_____
_____
_____
_____
_____
_____
_____
_____
_____
_____
_____
_____
_____
_____
_____
_____
_____
_____
_____
_____
_____
_____
_____
_____
_____
_____
_____
_____

Chapter Thirty-Seven

Chapter thirty-seven deals with feasts of 'Holy Convocation', including the Sabbath, the Feast of Trumpets, the Day of Atonement, the Feast of Tabernacles, Passover, the Feast of Unleavened Bread, and the Feast of Harvest or Weeks.

The blare of seven trumpets, as recorded in the book of Revelation is also discussed.

<u>The Sabbath</u> – *Leviticus 23: 1-4* – *"And the Lord spake unto Moses, saying,*

Speak unto the children of Israel and say unto them, Concerning the feasts of the Lord, which ye shall proclaim to be holy convocations, even these are my feasts.

Six days shall work be done: but the seventh day is the sabbath of rest, an holy convocation; ye shall do no work therein: it is the Sabbath of the Lord in all your dwellings.

These are the feasts of the Lord, even holy convocations, which ye shall proclaim in their seasons."

<u>Passover</u> – *Leviticus 23: 5* – *"In the fourteenth day of the first month at even is the Lord's Passover.*

<u>Unleavened Bread</u> *– Leviticus 23: "And on the fifteenth day of the same month is the feast of unleavened bread unto the Lord: seven days ye must eat unleavened bread.*

<u>Feast of Harvest or Weeks (Pentecost)</u> *– Leviticus – 23: 15-21 – "And ye shall proclaim on the selfsame day, that it may be an holy convocation unto you: ye shall do no servile work therein: it shall be for ever in your dwellings throughout your generations"*

Approximately 50 days – seven Sabbath weeks' worth - beginning in Passover, the Jews gave thanks to the Lord for the bountiful fruits of the harvest he had bestowed on them; they set aside additional periods of time to worship God; they provided food for the poor, and made sacrifices of burnt offerings to the Lord.

This joyful period of worship and thanksgiving culminates in the establishment of another feast of Holy Convocation as recorded above.

<u>Feast of Trumpets</u> - <u>*Leviticus 23: 23-25*</u> *- "Speak unto the children of Israel, saying,"*

In the seventh month, in the first day of the month, shall ye have a sabbath, a memorial of blowing of <u>trumpets</u>, a holy convocation."

Ye shall do no servile work therein: but ye shall offer an offering made by fire unto the Lord."

God established The Feast of Trumpets as a "holy convocation", a day of rest and a day wherein the blowing of trumpets is done as a memorial.

The Feast of Trumpets is celebrated on the first day of the seventh month (Tishri) of the Jewish Religious calendar (September/October), and is the New Year of the Jewish civil calendar, called Rosh Hashanah. (sta) 8 and 9, previously featured in Chapter Two of this book, are repeated below to reinforce the importance of this feast.

(sta) 8. - God established the Feast of Trumpets as a special memorial feast day. But its innate importance in sacred scripture is not yet fully recognized and appreciated.

(sta) 9. – The Feast of Trumpets is the linchpin of God's sacred feast days; days of holy convocations, days of sacred gatherings.

Although God did not designate a specific name for this feast, it evolved from being referred to as "The day of the sounding of the Ram's Horn" to "The Feast of 'Trumpets." The trumpet's blare signals the beginning of the Jewish civil new year.

Due to its unique positioning and functions in sacred Scripture, the Feast of Trumpets rightfully deserves to be considered as the lynchpin on which God's sacred feast days of Holy convocations hinge.

At God's command the first day of the seventh month of the Jewish religious calendar is designated as the first day of the Jewish civil calendar.

And this first day of the civil calendar is decreed by God to be a day of "holy convocation", a day of rest and a day wherein the blowing of trumpets is done as a memorial.

Here God established The Feast of Trumpets as a day of "holy convocation", a day of rest, a day wherein the blowing of trumpets is done as a memorial.

The Feast of Trumpets is celebrated on the first day of the seventh month (Tishri) of the Jewish Religious calendar (September/October), and is the New Year of the Jewish civil calendar. (Rosh Hashanah)

The Day of Atonement – *Leviticus 23: 27 – "Also on the tenth day of this seventh month there shall be a day of atonement: it shall be an holy convocation unto you; and ye shall afflict your souls, and offer an offering made by fire unto the Lord."*

The Feast of Tabernacles – *Leviticus – 23: 33-35 –"And the Lord spoke into Moses, saying,*

Speak unto the children of Israel, saying, The fifteenth day of this seventh month shall be the feast of tabernacles for seven days unto the Lord.

On the first day shall be an holy convocation: ye shall do no servile work therein."

The Feast of Tabernacles is the final feast of the seven feasts of holy convocation.

The Feast of Trumpets not only has reference to the Rapture of the Church, (see Paul's first letter to the Corinthians and first letter to the Thessalonians, below) but also has a prophetic reference to Israel. – (see Isaiah, immediately below:

<u>*In Isaiah 27:12 and 13*</u>, the Lord promises Israel:

"And it shall come to pass in that day, that the Lord shall beat off from the channel of the river unto the stream of Egypt, and ye shall be gathered one by one, O ye children of Israel."

"And it shall come to pass in that day, that the great <u>trumpet</u> shall be blown, and they shall come which we were ready to perish in the land of Assyria, and the outcasts in the land of Egypt, and shall worship the Lord in the holy mount at Jerusalem."*

* - It appears here that thru the prophet Isaiah, the Lord foretells the re-gathering of the Jews from the Diaspora – (the dispersion of the Jews to other nations), and that the trumpet will blare of their return to the temple at Jerusalem.

(sta) 135. - The trumpet's great blare will signal the return of the Jews to their promised land, and to their holy city Jerusalem, and the temple there.

The Feast of Trumpets (Rosh Ha Shana, New Year) harkens back to the ancient days of Israel, and looks ahead to our Redeemer's return. The blowing of the trumpet signifies the Rapture of the Church to its home in Heaven, and the calling of Israel back to its home in the Promised Land and to her capital Jerusalem. Let the trumpet blow.

How fitting it is that when Jesus next returns, descending on the clouds of heaven to meet His Raptured Church, heavenly trumpets will sound. In the following two Epistles, 1 Corinthians and 1 Thessalonians, Paul expounds on this important subject:

<u>1 Corinthians 15:51-58</u> – "Behold, I show you a mystery; We shall not all sleep, but we shall all be changed,

In a moment, in the twinkling of an eye, at the last <u>trump</u>: for the trumpet shall sound, and the dead shall be raised incorruptible, and we shall be changed.

For this corruptible must put on incorruption, and this mortal must put on immortality. So when this corruptible shall have put on incorruption, and this mortal shall have put on immortality, then shall be brought to pass the saying that is written, Death is swallowed up; in victory.

O death where is thy sting? O grave where is thy victory?

The sting of death is sin; and the strength of sin is the law.

But thanks be to God, which giveth us the victory through our Lord Jesus Christ.

Therefore my beloved brethren, be ye steadfast, unmovable, always abounding in the work of the Lord, forasmuch as ye know that your labor is not in vain in the Lord."

<u>1 Thessalonians 4: 13-18</u> – "But I would not have you to be ignorant, brethren, concerning them which are asleep, that ye sorrow not, even as others which have no hope.

For if we believe that Jesus died and rose again, even so them also which sleep in Jesus will God bring with him,

For this we say unto you by the word of the Lord, that we which are alive and remain unto the coming of the Lord shall not prevent them which are asleep.

For the Lord himself shall descend from heaven with a shout, with the voice of the archangel, and with the trump of God: and the dead in Christ shall rise first.

Then we which are alive and remain shall be caught up together with them in the clouds. To meet the Lord in the air: and so shall we ever be with the Lord.

Wherefore comfort one another with these words."

(sta) 136. – Before the great and terrible 'Tribulation', the believers who sleep and those alive at that time will awaken to the voice of the archangel and the trump of the Lord to meet with Jesus on the clouds of heaven.

And then, as revealed in Matthew 24: 29-31, recorded below, at the end of the Great Tribulation, God's angels will sound the trumpets. How many angels blaring how many trumpets, we do not know, but sacred Scripture tells us that the sound will be great:

<u>*Matthew 24: 29-31*</u>

"Immediately after the tribulation of those days shall the sun be darkened, and the moon shall not give her light, and the stars shall fall from heaven, and the powers of the heavens shall be shaken.

And then shall appear the sign of the Son of man in heaven; and then shall all the tribes of the earth mourn, and they shall see the Son of man coming in the clouds of heaven with power and great glory. And he shall send his angels with a great sound of a trumpet, and they shall gather together his elect from the four winds, from one end of heaven to the other."

(sta) 137. – Accompanied by the great sound of a trumpet, God's angels will gather His elect – (those deemed to be worthy of special favor, and special service to God) Thereafter, the seven trumps of judgment revealed in Revelation will recorded sound the seven judgments of the Lord.

Revelation, the final book of the Holy Bible, (to which no additions or subtractions are needed or authorized) informs us of the seven angels who will sound seven trumpets, pronouncing and activating seven judgments of the Lord:

Revelation 8: 7-8, 10, 12; 9: 1, 13-14; 10: 7; 11: 15

8: 7-8 – *"The first angel sounded, and there followed hail and fire mingled with blood, and they were cast upon the earth: and the third part of trees was burnt up, and all green grass was burnt up.*

And the second angel sounded, and as it were a great mountain burning with fire was cast into the sea, and the third part of the sea became blood."

8: 10 – *"And the third angel sounded, and there fell a great star from heaven, burning as it were a lamp, and it fell upon the third part of the rivers, and upon the fountains of waters"*

8: 12 – *And the fourth angel sounded, and the third part of the sun was smitten, and the third part of the moon, and the third part of the stars so as the third part of them was* darkened, and the day shone not for a third part of it, and the night likewise."

9: 1 – "And the fifth angel sounded, and I saw a star fall from haven unto the earth, and to him was given the key to the bottomless pit."

<u>9: 13-14</u> – "And the sixth angel sounded, and I heard a voice from the four horns of the golden altar which is before God,

Saying to the sixth angel which had the trumpet, Loose the four angels which are bound in the great river Euphrates."

10: 7 – "But in the days of the voice of the seventh angel, when he shall begin to sound, the mystery of God should be finished, as he hath declared to his servants the prophets."

11: 15 – "And the seventh angel sounded, and there were great voices in heaven, saying, The kingdoms of this world are become the kingdoms of our Lord, and of his Christ; and he shall reign for ever and ever."

(sta) 138. – "Trumpets are significantly associated with God's judgments.

(sta) 139. – Trumpets are significantly associated with God's kingship over heaven and earth, over the spiritual and physical.

And so ends Chapter Thirty-seven

Chapter Thirty-seven yields five significant trumpet associations:

(sta) 135. - The trumpet's great blare will signal the return of the Jews to their promised land, to their holy city Jerusalem, and the temple there.

(sta) 136. – Before the great and terrible 'Tribulation', the believers who sleep and those alive at that time will awaken to the voice of the archangel and the trump of the Lord to meet with Jesus on the clouds of heaven.

(sta) 137. – Accompanied by the great sound of a trumpet, God's angels will gather His elect –(those deemed to be worthy of special favor and special service to God) Thereafter, the seven trumps of judgment revealed in Revelation will recorded sound the seven judgments of the Lord.

(sta) 138. – "Trumpets are significantly associated with God's judgments.

(sta) 139. – Trumpets are significantly associated with God's kingship over heaven and earth, over spiritual and physical.

A partial analysis of those verses of scripture recorded in the Bible that indicate significant trumpet association of trumpets with the themes truths, lessons, and commandments of the Bible, reveal numerous such associations, including the following twenty broad categories:

1. – It is God's intention that mankind obey His commands and live in accordance with the divine plan for Salvation.

2. – Mankind needs God.

3. – The culmination of obedience to God's will are spiritual rewards a hundredfold more valuable than any possible temporal ones.

4. - At the end of this world, Jesus will reap that which He has sown, the harvest of His church consisting of those believers who have gone to their rest awaiting His return, and those believers who are alive when Jesus next comes again.

5. – The truly righteous are truly saved.

6. – The Son of Man came to save those of us who are lost, to offer salvation to the worldly, the recalcitrant and the otherwise, purposely blind.

7. – Unspoken specifically, but clearly indicated by Jesus' expressed desire to save the lost, less skepticism of those persons burdened with bad reputations who subsequently claim to have seen the light, is indicated.

8. – Our God is the God of creation, our God is the Word of God, and our God is the Spirit of God.

9. – God is not to be trifled with.

10. – God's judgment is sure, true, and indisputable.

11. – The Jews are God's chosen people.

12. – In the bible, "harvest" refers to man's harvest of food, but more importantly, it speaks of the gathering of believers by Jesus to companion with Him in the Kingdom of Heaven.

13. - Passover, the holy feast instituted by God celebrates the escape of the Jews from Egypt and their freedom from God's wrath directed at the Pharaoh and his people. Passover signals the beginning of the Jewish civil year.

14. The genealogy of Jesus as established by Matthew, traces the kingly ancestry of Joseph (His adoptive father) from king David to Jesus.

15. - The genealogy of Jesus established by Luke backtracks Jesus ancestry from Joseph, his adoptive father, to Adam, the created Son of God.

16. – Jesus is the rightful heir to the throne of Israel.

17. – Throughout the Bible, Trump, Trumpet, Trumpeter, Trumpets are significantly associated with Salvation.

18. – As demonstrated in Paul's hazardous journeys to spread the Gospel of Jesus the Christ, the Apostles exhibited extraordinary bravery and trust in God.

19. – Trumpets are closely associated with wars, the physical and spiritual cost of wars, the armies of war, the conduct of war, and with the outcome of various battles.

20. – Our God is one God, made known to us in three manifestations.

Are you listening? The sound is very faint, and as yet, is only one. But it will grow in number and in volume. Despite how slight the sound, you can hear it now. Take heart. Do not think it an illusion. Our Lord Jesus Christ, the only begotten Son of God the Father, born of the blessed virgin Mary, the adopted son of Joseph the carpenter; He who was born in Bethlehem and raised in Nazareth, (the Nazarene) our perfect man and perfect God will come again. This time He does not travel quietly with little public notice.

This time he arrives with fanfare, with the blare of trumpets heard 'round the world and across His boundless universe, heard with joy within the hearts and souls of all those who stayed the course, who loved Him beyond their love of selves.

This time Jesus comes to take us to a better place, a place where justice and peace prevail, a place without tears, a place without stress. This time our Heavenly Father comes to bring us home.

Listen for the trumpet sound. It will come; softly at first, but it will come.

And so ends this book, "Softly Now The Trumpet".

Notes and Reflections

To the reader:

Thank you for your time, your patience, and your understanding.

May this book be a blessing to you.

May the inspiration that guided me in this endeavor transform my poor literary skills into words of wisdom that whisper in your ear, stimulate your intellect, and motivate you to read the Bible.

May all of us gain a greater love and appreciation of Jesus Christ, perfect man and perfect God.

I can think of no better way to end this book than by quoting Matthew 22: 34-40:

Matthew 22: 34-40

"But when the Pharisees had heard that he had put the Sadducees to silence, they were gathered together.

Then one of them which was a lawyer, asked him a question, tempting him, and saying,

Master, which is the great commandment in the law?

Jesus said unto him,

Thou shalt love thy God with all thy heart, and with all thy soul, and with all thy mind.

This is the first and great commandment.

And the second is like unto it, Thou shalt love thy neighbor as thyself.

On these two commandments hang all the law and the prophets."

With peace and love in my heart, I humbly pray that God may bless you and yours.

Goodbye,

Frank Connelly

Thank You

To: Anne, my editor, most steadfast supporter, my best friend, and my wife.

To: Our four sons: Frank, Danny, Patrick, and Jerry, whose love and encouragement never fail.

To: Our daughter Catherine who always has a good word to say and a constructive suggestion to make. Getting old is not easy, but Catherine helps ease the way.

To: Catherine's husband Tom Del Grosso who comes to the rescue when I have computer problems.

And a quick shout-out to eleven of the world's best grandchildren:

Brian, Cally, Christine, Keith, Kevin, Kristen, Lara, Michael, Ryan, Sean, and Shannon.

This book is dedicated to a boyhood friend, Gerard Henrich who was killed in action in Korea.

About The Author

Born and raised in Brooklyn, New York, the author is 83 yrs. of age as of this writing. Frank is a veteran of the Korean War; having served fourteen months there as a member of the Army Security Agency.

In 1975, after a career lasting twenty years, Frank retired as a Lieutenant from the New York City Police Department. He first put 'pen to paper' late in life when his daughter

Catherine, and her husband Tom presented him with a computer on his 70th birthday.

"Softly Now The Trumpet" is his fifth book. The first two books were autobiographical; the next two were about Jesus, as is this one. Frank says that if he lives long enough to write another book, it too will be about Jesus. "There is no better, more interesting person or subject matter to spend words on than Jesus, the humble son of a humble carpenter. Jesus is the perfect man to emulate, and the perfect God to worship."

Printed in the United States
By Bookmasters